Best Wishes

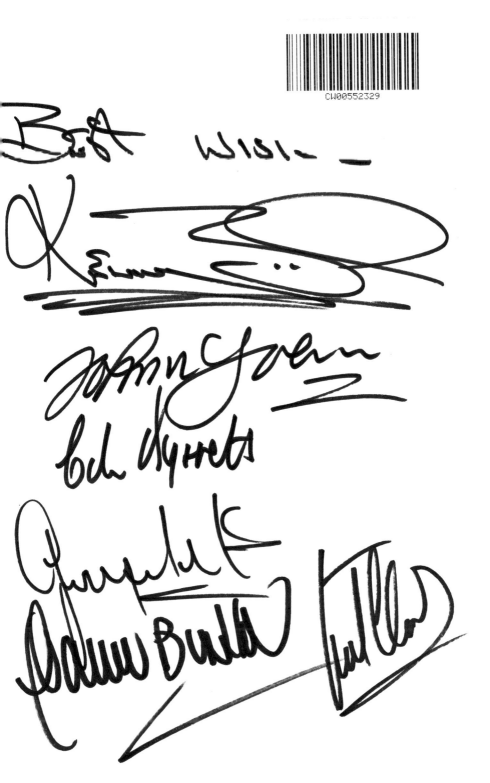

Kenny Burns

No ifs or butts

With Ray Yeomans

First published in November 2009

*Pictures courtesy of the Nottingham Evening Post, Derby Telegraph, Birmingham Post,
PA, Action Images and John Sumpter
Acknowledgements: Ivan Barnsley, John Lawson, Danny Boyes, Duncan Payne*

*Printed in Great Britain by Hickling & Squires Limited, Unit 1, Engine Lane, Moorgreen
Business Park, Moorgreen, Nottingham NG16 3QU*

Published by Kenny Burns Promotions

This book is a limited edition, of
which this is number:

Foreword

By Viv Anderson

I feel honoured to be asked to write the foreword to this book because Kenny and I go back a long way. We were all shocked when Forest signed Kenny from Birmingham because he was a striker. Yet the bosses must have spotted something special in him because they converted him to a defender to play alongside Larry Lloyd. They felt that not much would get past that pair – and they were right. They gelled very quickly and were absolutely superb together for almost four years.

When I first broke into the first team at the City Ground I was only on about £50 a week and couldn't afford a car. So Kenny, who also lived in Clifton used to give me a lift to training.

He used to have a stop watch next to the steering wheel and would time how long it took to drop his daughter off at the nursery. He drove at a million miles an hour to try and knock a couple of seconds off his time. He was like Stirling Moss when he got behind the wheel and he scared me to death.

I used to get my own back on away trips because Tony Woodcock and myself used to ambush him. We'd get the key to his room and jump on him when he least expected it. We'd sit on him, hold him down and take his teeth out. It was a bit like Inspector Clouseau and Kato. He knew it was coming but he wasn't quite sure when.

He has the image of a hard man but believe me, he does have a gentle side. He's also got a dry sense of Scottish humour, a bit like another good friend of mine, Gordon McQueen.

How good was Kenny? Well, good enough to play for his country 20 times. Good enough to win two European Cups.

A great striker of the ball, he could do a job for you in attack, midfield or defence. He was also a great team player. If you were in trouble, the first person you would turn to was Kenny.

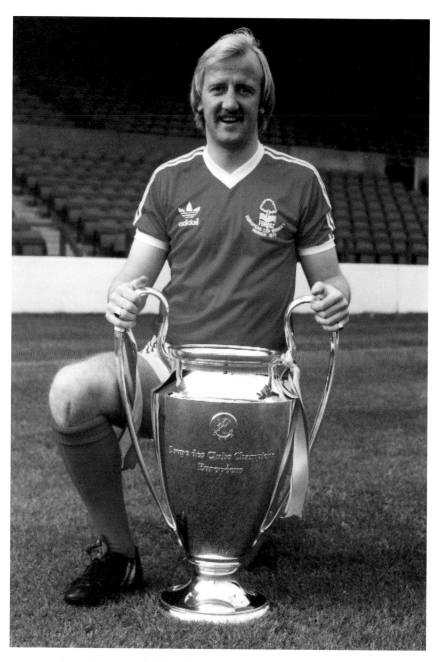

A proud moment - holding the most prestigious club cup in the world

Introduction

WHEN I was a lad football was a man's game, played by men. Not like today. I struggle to watch a full match these days, I really do. I don't even bother with internationals, especially friendlies. I'll probably watch five minutes at a time and then flick channels.

I'd much rather sit and watch a video of one of our old games. Why? Because football is not a sport these days, it's just a business.

There is a lot of money floating around now, but some clubs are being run poorly. Money talks and I'm afraid the game's gone crazy. The monopoly money some players are being paid is obscene.

Having said that, I still think English football is the best in the world. The Italians have good technical skills, don't get me wrong, but they are more worried about how their hair looks and showing off their latest tattoo than how they play. I couldn't watch Italian football every week, that's for sure.

We had some truly great nights of European football at Forest. But it's not the same these days is it? Why have seeding? What's that all about? The last European match I went to was Rangers v Roma. Rangers lost 3-0 and the centre-forward stood about so long that he must have put on 5lb in weight. It was a disgrace.

The fact is, some of today's players don't know they are born. They are wrapped in cotton wool. Quite simply, Ronaldo and co, good as they are, would not have survived in my day.

They are over-paid and pampered. They have everything done for them from an early age. They would even have their arses wiped in the dressing room before a match if you let them.

They are spoilt to death, with their Porsches and baby Bentleys, designer suites, diamond earrings and Rolex watches. There are some good players out there, don't get me wrong. But there are many, earning millions who are just ordinary – they just have good engines.

Let's face it, some of them are just tarts. If they ladder their stockings they're out for six weeks. Not that it bothers them – because they are still dragging in more in a week than the Prime

Minister does in a year. They think they are great players – but let me tell you, they're not.

Great players are Denis Law, Pele, John Charles, George Best, Dave Mackay and Jim Baxter. Now, they are great players.

Jim was probably the most gifted player of his generation. He was world class yet he only earned £45 a week when he was at Rangers. What would he be worth on today's market?

A lot of players today don't even know how to tackle properly. I was taught from a very early age not to go on your arse; stay on your feet; don't dive in. Bryan Robson was one of the best at that.

But the authorities have turned football into a game for pansies.

If certain players do get tackled they dive and roll over and over as if they've been shot by a sniper. Give me a break, I've seen more physical contact at Tesco.

Players pretend to be injured to try and get the opposition booked, or even better, sent off. It's despicable. They are cheats.

And don't even get me started on agents and imaging rights. What's that all about? Peter Shilton and Trevor Francis had agents. What for? I thought sod off, you're not getting any of my money. Some agents, who have made millions out of the game, have never even kicked a football. Just what do they do to earn their money? The game would be better off without them.

Another thing wrong with today's game is that there are too many coaches filling players' heads with too many tactics, especially at dead-ball situations.

A former international player recently told me they had 20 different routines at free-kicks at his club. Why make it so complicated? At Forest we had two routines at free-kicks – tap it to one side or shoot. And you know what, it worked.

Football is a very simple game. Mark a man and make sure he doesn't score. It's basic. Win the ball, pass the ball, stick it in the net. Simple.

Brian Clough used to say: "The ball never gets tired. Let the ball do the work." As usual, he was dead right. He wasn't wrong very often.

The gaffers used to drum it into us at Forest that if we gave a sloppy pass away early doors we would be sloppy for the rest of the 90 minutes. The same went for your first tackle.

I've performed at places like Wembley, Barcelona and the Olympic stadium in front of crowds of 100,000. And I've played non-league from Ilkeston to Grantham in front of one man and a dog. I've done it all. I've even helped put the nets up on a Sunday morning. I've played at all levels and made sure I enjoyed it because, after all, you're a long time dead...

I was considered to be hard. But I like to think I was fair… most of the time. But if a centre-forward was knocking lumps off me I was going to give him some back wasn't I? When someone elbowed me slyly in the mouth, I would bide my time and pay him back.

I never set out to deliberately hurt anyone and, as far as I know, I never had any enemies out there. But when I went into a 50-50 tackle I thought 'better them than me' if anyone did get hurt. It's human nature, isn't it? Show me one footballer who doesn't try to get away with something on the pitch? A nudge at a corner, a grab of the shirt in the penalty area. It's part and parcel of the game. Some Italians and South Americans may even claim it is a skill.

If a player said I was a hard bastard I would take it as a compliment. It showed I was doing my job.

I've come up against some really hard men over the years, but nobody really frightened me.

Stoke's Denis Smith and Alan Bloor were tough. So were Graeme Souness and Jimmy Case at Liverpool. I once caught Jimmy a good one on his knee. He got up and didn't even rub the injury. I saw the look in his eye and ran over to the gaffer and said "I think ma hamstring's gone."

I also admired Norman Hunter, Jackie Charlton, Paul Madeley and Billy Bremner at Leeds and Johnny Giles could be a bit tasty when he wanted to.

But centre-halves are a different breed of man. They are born braver and stronger than the rest of us and I don't think they feel pain in the same way. Men like Micky Droy (Chelsea), John Roberts (Arsenal), Stuart Boam (Middlesbrough), John McGrath (Southampton) – now they were hard.

Mick Harford (Luton) was tough and I had many a battle with my old mate Joe Jordan. But we weren't mates once the front teeth came out and I went to work.

Andy Gray was always a handful, but I think strikers work best in pairs. And in Gray and John Richards Wolves had two of the best. Richards was a very intelligent player, very difficult to mark

Yes, I got booked a lot, but I wasn't sent off that often. And when I was it was usually for swearing at referees. I think they had it in for me.

Yes I was a hard player, but you had to know how to look after yourself in those days. You had to be a wee bit ruthless. You couldn't let a centre-forward or a centre-half get away with knocking lumps off you.

I tried to keep within the laws… if I didn't, too bad. Brian Clough felt that if you were going to get booked you might as well make it for something worthwhile. If you gave someone a clout early on they might think "I don't fancy that" and drift off to the wing. Brian Little at Villa was like that. And the classic example was Kevin Keegan in the European Cup final between Forest and Hamburg. He got whacked a few times and almost ended up playing full-back.

I had a wee bit of a reputation, on and off the field. But I don't think I was a particularly dirty player. I did have a temper though, especially in the early days.

Once, in a practice match a young lad, I think his name was Simon Worthington, stuck the ball through my legs. I said: "Do that again and I'll butt you." The cheeky little bugger did it again so I stuck the head on him and walked away. Looking back it's not something I'm proud of. But I did warn him…

Unlike today's millionaire players with their flash cars, mansions and Page 3 girlfriends, I never made a fortune out of the game. And fame never changed me. I still like a pint, a frame of snooker and a round of golf.

I'm still just Kenny. Nothing special. I never tried to be something I wasn't. I knew my limits. I knew what I could and couldn't do. There were times after I retired when I was skint. They were dark times, believe me.

I was only four minutes down the road from Brian Clough, but I never turned to him. I never begged or borrowed. If I hadn't got enough money for a drink I would have a glass of water and make out I was on a diet. I just tried to put on a brave face and kept my chin up.

No one likes to be shit on in any walk of life and I've been shit on many times. I've been married three times... and banned from driving three times... and lived in a modest house near Derby. So do I envy the likes of John Terry on 150 grand a week? Bloody right I do. But, I'm not bitter. Honest!!

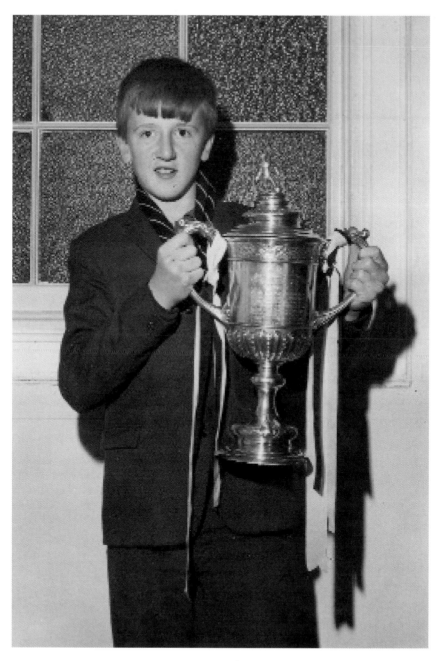

I get my hands on the Scottish Cup during a trip to a local social club

Once a Ranger always a Ranger

It will shock some people to discover that I was born Kenneth Maguire in Camlachie in Glasgow on September 23, 1953. The address on my birth certificate says 253 Duke Street, but I've never been back there. I was adopted as a baby, but it never bothered me and I never tried to find out who my real parents were. I never had the urge. I still don't.

The truth is, I had a happy childhood and was brought up by a wonderful lady, Mary Burns, in a council house in Peat Road, in Glasgow, with my four brothers, James, Ed, Archie and Tommy and sisters Mammie, Anna and Jenny. Sadly, only Ed is still living. We still talk on the phone.

My mum died when I was 12. She was a character and, being the baby of the family, she spoiled me to death. But her word was law.

I never really wanted for anything and I lived with my brothers when she passed away. James, the oldest, was like a dad to me. Archie was in the Navy. Once he made my bed for me and the sheets were so tight that I couldn't get out at night to go to toilet. I peed the bed.

James did not really get on with Archie. But Archie got a right kicking once after going to help some mates in a fight. They ran off and left him and he ended up a right mess. He was in bed for about two weeks while he recovered. When his so-called mates finally came round to visit him my other brothers kicked the shit out of them.

Where we lived you either played football or you were in a gang. There wasn't much else to do, apart from watch my heroes at Rangers.

There were rough areas either side of us and you had to be a bit street-wise. I remember going into a chip shop and there were iron bars, with just enough space to pass a bottle of Irn Bru through. It was like Dodge City at times, especially on Friday and Saturday nights when the barmen kicked the drunks out into the streets.

But we were happy kicking a ball around all hours and just kept ourselves to ourselves. Boys will be boys, of course, but we never got into any real trouble. Jim Cannon, who went on to play for Crystal Palace, was one of my pals. I used to play with the bigger, older lads and filled in anywhere they were short.

I never had time for girls in those days, although I suppose my first sweetheart was a girl called Morag.

I played football at Burnbrae Primary School. I wasn't interested in any other sports really.

We used to play an hour and a half each way often staying out until ten or eleven at night, until the drunks started turning out and the fights started.

I played up front because, even then, I wanted to score goals. A lad called Bobby Hutchinson and me were the best players. We got to two finals and won them both. We were used to playing on ash pitches but we got to play on grass in the final. Luxury.

I liked school, especially maths. One year my brother James – who wanted me to be an architect – said he would give me a couple of quid if I did well in the next maths test.

Unfortunately, I was at the dentists that day and missed the start. But I whizzed through it and finished top of the class. But the following year I was crap. We had a new teacher and I couldn't understand a word he said.

My brothers played for Gregor United and I used to clean their boots. In those days they used to drink about five pints – and that was before a game!

I stopped playing for the school because we had our own team, Hillwood Boys Club, who produced ex-internationals like Alex McLeish and Tommy Coyne.

Then I played for the 58th Boys Brigade under Staff Sergeant Willie Smith, who also lived on Peat Road. He was a plumber, who was football daft and took us training at a school every Tuesday and Thursday. We scored a record 126 goals in ten games and only conceded five. Bobby Hutchinson got 40 of those, including eleven in one match which we won 30-0.

Junior football is very big in Scotland and we thought we were super-stars when we got our team picture in the Daily Record.

I was doing well until I broke my leg playing in goal in a five-a-side game. That's how I learned to kick with my left leg. I used to play in goal even with my leg in plaster, I was that keen … or daft.

I left school at 16 and I was determined that I wasn't going to work in a factory. That would have killed me. I wanted to be in the fresh air and fancied a job as a green keeper at the local golf club.

I was playing for Glasgow Amateurs by then. They were a good club and Willie Donachie started out there.

My big break came when Rangers, the club I supported (I still do), asked me to go for a trial. I knew I had arrived when the scout picked me up in an Hillman Minx (taxed).

I was a massive Rangers fan, always will be. They offered me £5 a week, training twice a week, but I turned it down. Turned down the chance to join the likes of Jim Baxter, my hero, and wee Willie Henderson. Mad eh?

When I told my brothers they didn't talk to me for a fortnight. But I knew what I wanted …£10 and an apprenticeship. Eventually I got my way and was signed on 'S'forms by William Thornton. And I loved it.

I didn't mind cleaning boots and the toilets and sweeping up. But the closest I got to a ball was giving it a coat of dubbin.

I was playing for Glasgow Amateurs and the Rangers third team. But I got sent off three times for Amateurs, once for head-butting someone. I can't remember why, perhaps I didn't like his face.

I was always in trouble with referees and getting banned. But that didn't stop me. I would just play under an assumed name – Smith. Our manager was Willie Smith and we also had a Sammy and a Gordon, so one more Smith didn't make much difference. I think half the lads didn't play under their own name.

I had such a temper that I was flaring up all the time. I ended up banned for four months and that didn't go down too well at Ibrox.

I played against Glasgow Transport and Glasgow University at the Albion training ground, along with Alex Ferguson, in front of two men and a dog. But I only played a couple of games for Rangers before they called me in and said they didn't think I had a future there after all. But at least I had worn the shirt – and that was a great honour.

It was a body blow. But, in life, you need lows to help you appreciate the highs.

Rangers said they would do their best to help get me fixed up. But nothing happened. It was the end of the world … Shit, I would have to get a job after all.

But two weeks later, out of the blue, I was offered a week-long trial at Manchester City with Frankie Gray and three other lads from Glasgow, Joe O'Connor, Ian Fitzgerald and Joe Welsh.

Managed by Joe Mercer and Malcolm Allison, City had a good team then, with the likes of Colin Bell, Mike Doyle, Joe Corrigan and Mike Summerbee. Ian Bowyer was a teenage winger there. But they never took us on.

A week later I got a call that Birmingham City were interested in giving me a two-week trial. Unbelievably, the following day Crystal Palace also came calling.

I stayed at the Moat House Hotel with O'Connor - who was a right pain in the arse, by the way. I played in a trial game at Birmingham with Joe and they must have liked what they saw because they said they would like to sign both of us. It was the start of a great journey.

They were great days. Happy days. Some of the best of my life … and that includes winning European Cups with Nottingham Forest.

Forest or Birmingham? I couldn't choose between the two. I still look out for their results – as I do with every club I played for.

Burns family gathering

Top of the class. I'm pictured with John Crawley, Doug Barber, Dave Smith, Andrew Whitlock, Harry Lawrie, Boyd Greer, Sam Smith, Gordon Connelly, Robert Hutchinson, James Jeffrey.

Scottish Amateur Football Association

4 WEEKS

AFFILIATED TO THE SCOTTISH FOOTBALL ASSOCIATION, LIMITED

5 Southview Crescent.
Bridge of Weir

Kennell. Burns.
16. 1. 70.

Dear Sir, Please attend a meeting of the Youth.
Committee. To Be held at the SFA Rooms 6 Park Gardens
Glasgow C3. on Friday 23.1.70 at 7.55
Re being ordered off in the Game v Boakle on
Saturday 20.12.69. For Attempting to Butt an
opponent.

Should you be enable to attend. Please send me
your defence in writing.

Failure to appear or send a defence. your case. will
be heard in your Absence.

Yours Sincerely
W McPhee.
Ass Youth Secy

Summoned to an SAFA disciplinary hearing after being sent off in 1969

SCOTTISH AMATEUR FOOTBALL LEAGUE.
6 Bothlin Drive, Stepps, Glasgow.E.3.

Dear Sir,   2 MAR 1970

Mosspark Y.C.   V   Glasgow Ams.

17 1 /70.

In respect of your having been ordered from the field of play
during the course of the above game for deliberately kicking an
opponent.   , I have to confirm/
advise the decision of the Executive Committee Meeting held on
                  that you have been suspended from all participation
in football from   2 MAR 1970   until   12 APR 1970

                              Yours faithfully,
                              ROBERT GILMOUR.
                              Hon. Secretary.
Kenneth Burns, Esq.,
279 Peat Road, Glasgow.S.W.2.

Facing a lengthy ban....

SCOTTISH AMATEUR FOOTBALL LEAGUE.
6 Bothlin Drive, Stepps, Glasgow.E.3.   2 MAR 1970

Dear Sir,

Glasgow Ams.   V   Kilmarnock Ams.

24/ 1 /70.

In respect of your having been ordered from the field of play
during the course of the above game for deliberately kicking
an opponent   , I have to confirm/
advise the decision of the Executive Committee Meeting held on
                  that you have been suspended from all participation
in football from   12 APR 1970   until   31 MAY 1970

                              Yours faithfully,
                              ROBERT GILMOUR.
                              Hon. Secretary.
Kenneth Burns, Esq.
279 Peat Road,
Glasgow.S.W.2.

But it didn't stop me. I played under an assumed name

An Agreement made the 14th

day of August 19 70 between Alan Gilbert Instone

of St. Andrew's, Birmingham 9

in the COUNTY OF Warwickshire

the Secretary of and acting pursuant to Resolution and Authority for and on

behalf of the BIRMINGHAM CITY FOOTBALL CLUB

of St. Andrew's, Birmingham 9 (hereinafter referred to as the Club)

of the one part and KENNETH BURNS

of 279 Peat Road, Glasgow

in the COUNTY OF Lanarkshire Apprentice Football Player

(hereinafter referred to as the Player) of the other part Whereby it is agreed

as follows:—

1. The Player hereby agrees to play in an efficient manner and to the best of his ability for the Club.

2. The Player shall attend the Club's ground or any other place decided upon by the Club for the purposes of or in connection with his training as a Player pursuant to the instructions of the Secretary, Manager, or Trainer of the Club, or of such other person, or persons as the Club may appoint.

3. The Player shall do everything necessary to get and keep himself in the best possible condition so as to render the most efficient service to the Club, and will carry out all the training and other instructions of the Club through its representative officials.

4. The Player shall observe and be subject to all the Rules, Regulations and Bye-Laws of The Football Association, and any other Association, League, or Combination of which the Club shall be a member. And this Agreement shall be subject to any action which shall be taken by The Football Association under their Rules for the suspension or termination of the Football Season, and if any such suspension or termination shall be decided upon the payment of wages shall likewise be suspended or terminated, as the case may be.

5. The Player shall not engage in any business or live in any place which the Directors (or Committee) of the Club may deem unsuitable, provided that the Club shall, at the request of the Player or his Parent or Guardian, allow the Player to continue his further education or take up suitable vocational training.

6. If the Player shall be guilty of serious misconduct or breach of the disciplinary Rules of the Club, the Club may, on giving 14 days' notice to the said Player, or the Club may, on giving 28 days' notice to the said Player, on any reasonable grounds, terminate this Agreement and dispense with the services of the Player in pursuance of the Rules of all such Associations, Leagues,

My first contract with the Blues...

10. In consideration of the observance by the said player of the terms, provisions and conditions of this Agreement, the said Alan Gilbert Instone on behalf of the Club hereby agrees that the said Club shall pay to the said Player the sum of £ 8.0.0. per week from 14th August 1970 to 22nd September 1971

and £ per week from

to and £ per week from

to

and £ per week from

to and £ per week from

to

11. This Agreement (subject to the Rules of The Football Association) shall cease and determine on 22nd September 1971 unless the same shall have been previously determined in accordance with the provisions hereinbefore set forth.

Fill in any
other pro-
visions
required

Match bonuses as per rule.

As Witness the hands of the said parties the day and year first aforesaid

Signed by the said Alan Gilbert Instone

and Kenneth Burns

k Burns

(Player)

In the presence of the Parent or Guardian of the Player

(Signature) James Burns

(Occupation) Sheet Iron Worker

(Address) 279 Peat Rd

Glasgow SW3

A.G. Instone

(Secretary)

...Witnessed by my brother, James

BIRMINGHAM CITY FOOTBALL CLUB LTD.

SECRETARY - A. G. INSTONE
MANAGER- ~~STANLEY~~ F. GOODWIN
TELEPHONES: 021-772 0101
2699
TELEGRAMS "MERIKEN, BIRMINGHAM"

REGISTERED OFFICE AND GROUND

St. Andrew's Ground

Birmingham, 9

DD/SF

11th August 1970

Mr. J. Burns,
279 Peat Road,
Nitsill,
Glasgow, S.W.3.

Dear Mr. Burns,

　　　　Regarding our telephone conversation of Monday night,
please find enclosed Apprentice Forms.

　　　　You will note on each form I have marked where you have
to fill in the necessary details and underneath where you sign your
name you will note the date. Would you be sure to sign the forms and
date them for Friday, 14th August 1970. This will give me time
to receive the forms from you and get Ken to sign with the same date.
I have enclosed a S.A.E. for this purpose.

　　　　Would you also send <u>Ken's Birth Certificate</u> with these forms.

　　　　With very best wishes,

Yours sincerely,

D. Dorman
<u>Chief Scout</u>

ENC.

Taken on as an apprentice at Birmingham City

Manager F. GOODWIN
Secretary A. G. INSTONE

Registered Office and Ground
St. Andrew's Ground Birmingham— B9 4NH telephone. 021 772 0101/2689 telegrams "Heathen" Birmingham

Birmingham City
Football Club
Limited

28th June, 1971.

Mr. K. Burns,
279 Peat Road,
Glasgow, S.W.3.

Dear Ken,

I am authorised by the Manager, Mr. Goodwin, to offer you a full professional contract as and from the 1st July next for a period of one year plus a one year option.

Your basic wage during this period will be £18 per week plus £25 for each first team appearance together with the usual match bonus and incentive payments. In addition there would be the £250 signing on fee which would be paid to you in weekly payments over the period of your contract and option period, amounting to approximately £2.40 per week.

If you are agreeable to accepting these terms I would be pleased if you could let me know by return so that the necessary contracts may be drawn up and I am enclosing a stamped addressed envelope for your reply.

Yours sincerely,

A.G. Instone '
Secretary

My first professional contract - £18 a week!

The teenage Blue - me aged 18

Singing the Blues

Birmingham was a happy, friendly club with a great bunch of supporters. I had a sister living near Birmingham and I felt at home straight away. I've been back a few times and the memories came flooding back as soon as I walked into the ground. I still keep in touch with some of the old boys like Jimmy Calderwood. He reminded me of the day I nearly drowned him on a club trip to Martinique.

We had hired a dingy and the lads, unwisely, let me drive. Jimmy went overboard and I nearly chopped his head off with the propeller. When we moved on to Australia we had been drinking all night and broke into a place on the beach that had trampolines. We bounced along six in a row and then went splat – straight into a wall. We were out for the count. Bondi beach was special. I got hit by a wave that ripped my trunks, tore my wedding ring off my finger and I almost lost my teeth. Although that didn't kill me, the 25-hour flight back almost did. I don't like flying at the best of times.

I was at the local derby with Villa and although the fans were as passionate as ever, there didn't seem to be the same desire, commitment and passion out on the pitch.

I had a great rapport with the Birmingham fans who had seen me come through the youth team. They knew I was what it said on the can. They really took to me, I think, after I scored in the local derby at their old rivals Villa. I ran round Chris Nichol and put it past Jimmy Rimmer. After I scored I ran to the Holt End with my arms in the air. Boy, did that feel good.

I was also proud of my goal that helped us to a 2-2 draw against Manchester United at Old Trafford. There were 58,898 in there that day – with thousands more locked out.

I also enjoyed a 2-1 home win over our other big local rivals, Wolves. It was some match. We were a goal down after a minute and had keeper Gary Sprake carried off on his home debut.

Bob Latchford went in goal and made a great save and we equalised with a controversial penalty. I was pushed into the attack in place of Bob and scored the winner with a diving header, after good work by Gordon Taylor and Trevor Francis.

There were other memorable moments – like being voted Midland Player of the Year in 1974. I was only 20, but had already played sweeper in place of John Roberts; striker in place of Bob Hatton and Bob Latchford; centre-half in place of Roger Hynd and midfield in place of Malcolm Page. I felt very honoured to win the award – and the hundred quid that went with it, of course – and to follow in the footsteps of Don Howe, Gerry Hitchens, Tony Brown and John Richards.

The four goals I scored against Derby County in October 1976 obviously springs to mind – although I was convinced I only got a hat-trick until someone recently showed me a press cutting.

Struggling Derby, without a win under Dave Mackay, didn't have the greatest of sides then. Roy McFarland was out injured, but they still lined up with young Moseley on goal, Rod Thomas and David Nish at full-back, Peter Daniel and Colin Todd, Bruce Rioch, Henry Newton, Archie Gemmill, Tony Maken, Charlie George and Welsh international Leighton James.

Heavy rain before the kick-off made the surface treacherous but I'd grabbed a hat-trick before half time and got my fourth on 71 minutes. I also hit the bar and post.

We swept into the lead after only eight minutes. Jones raced down the wing and got over a perfect cross for me to steer a header into the net. A clever flick by Francis put Calderwood away and his cross-shot hit the woodwork and rebounded back into play. There was an empty net in front of me but I somehow managed to hit the bar.

I got another chance after 22 minutes after good work from Hibbitt and Francis and this time I beat the keeper with a low shot. Latchford saved well from Rioch and George shot over before I completed my hat-trick after 31 minutes. Styles put Francis away and I managed to side-foot his hard, low cross into the net – despite being off balance. The fans went mad and were chanting: "We want six." But it was Derby who pulled a goal back through James after a mistake by Latchford. The Rams caused a stir when they withdrew Todd, who wanted a transfer, at half-time and replaced him with Jeff King. We were also forced into a change because Joe Gallagher was injured. Gary Pendry came on with Want moving into defence. The Rams had the better of the early chances but Daniel was booked for pulling my shirt. And I got the better of him again after 71 minutes. He hesitated over a back pass and I nipped in to trickle the ball into the net.

In April 1974, I bagged my first League hat-trick in a 3-3 draw with Leicester, who had Peter Shilton in goal, after we had gone 2-0 down in front of a crowd of 28,486. It was certainly an eventful game for me. I was at fault when Cross opened the scoring in only the second minute. Back helping the defence, I failed to cut out a cross from the left and Cross chested the ball down in a crowded goalmouth and forced a low shot past Dave Latchford. Glover made it 2-0 after 19 minutes, but then I chased a long ball into the area and steered it past Shilton before stabbing it into the net.

I was causing Cross a few problems now and equalised with a real cracker. I chased a long ball from Campbell down the left, waited for it to bounce and volleyed a right-footer into the top corner before Shilts could move.

Four minutes after the break a Francis cross was headed down by Bob Hatton and I ran on to blast the ball past a stranded Shilton.

I also had a goal disallowed for off-side after I volleyed a Taylor cross just inside the near post and thought I had won us the game, but Len Glover equalised with his second.

Leicester had a good team in those days with Whitworth and Rofe at full-back, Weller, Sammels and Worthington and the tricky Glover on the wing.

The other game that springs to mind was at Leicester in December 1976. The frozen pitch that day wasn't great and there was a doubt about the match going ahead, but we turned it on and won 6-2. The result was never in doubt after Gary Emmanuel and Trevor Francis struck twice in two minutes.

I was in the middle of a real purple patch and the hat-trick of headers I grabbed that day won me a superb £3,300 TR7 sports car.

A Blues fan had pledged to give the car as an incentive to the Blues player scoring the sixth goal in a game. I had just missed it against Derby but it was mine this time. Not that I got to keep it. We split the money up between all the players – even the youth team got a few quid. And I got to go home in my old Austin 1100. When my mum died she left me £250 and I put it towards the car.

You had to know how to look after yourself in those days when the tackles came flying in. When we played Newcastle in the Texaco Cup Jinky Smith, who was their record signing from Aberdeen, did one of the latest tackles in the history of the game and Tony Want ended up with a broken leg. The game was held up for about 20 minutes. It was horrible. Jinky was a big crowd favourite and used to do tricks at half-time but he had to retire at 29 with knee injuries.

We were playing them in the league again on the Saturday and some of the lads were talking about getting revenge for Tony.

I caught Irvine Nattrass a good one on the knee but, fortunately, Clive 'The Book' Thomas was the referee and he waved play on. I didn't like referees, but I got on well with him to be fair.

Frank Clark was playing for Newcastle and he had a run in with Paul Hendrie and grabbed him by the throat. A few minutes later there was a 50/50 ball and Frank got stretchered off with a hole in his leg. I think he's still got the scar.

Coming from Scotland, I thought I could handle myself, but I was taught a harsh lesson in a game against Stoke, who had Denis Smith and Alan Bloor at the heart of the defence. To put it mildly, they didn't take any prisoners in those days. Quite simply, they kicked the shit out of me. I was head-butted and kicked up the arse. They kicked my shins and when I fell over they stood on my hands. But I wasn't going to take it lying down and made up my mind that I was going to pay one of them back. I didn't care which one, but I was having my revenge.

My chance came when Terry Hibbitt slipped a pass between Smith and Mike Pejic with about five minutes to go. I slowed up allowing Smith to try and shield the ball out for a goal kick and then jumped on the back of his legs. He said he was going to break my legs when he got up … but he couldn't move. "No I'm not I'm going to break both your legs, rip your head off and stick it up your arse."

He wasn't a happy man. Luckily the referee had come over to see what was going off. "Did you hear that ref?" I asked. He said "Yes, but I think he was talking to you."

On one occasion, Norwich City manager John Bond said I should have been sent off after clash with Ted McDougall and claimed one of his players was scared to go near me. But I didn't think I was dirty: I just played the game hard – the way it is meant to be played.

Sometimes it was me that came off worst. I was playing against Manchester City when their keeper, big Joe Corrigan, accidentally punched me on the nose. I could hardly remember anything – except the pain. I'd already bagged 14 goals that season so I was keen to carry on playing. My nose was broken but I played through the pain barrier for three games, including a 2-0 win over Sunderland, before going into hospital for an operation.

On another occasion John Deehan gave me a whack and I ended up whistling through a hole in my lip.

Freddie Goodwin was the manager when I arrived at Birmingham and in Sid Owen they had one of the best coaches around.

Tony Hateley had just left but they also had plenty of experienced players like Trevor Hockey, Geoff Vowden, Gary Pendry, Phil Summerill and Bob Latchford.

I'll never forget Hockey, he was like the Wolf Man. He even had a hairy car, covered in blue mohair, fitted with a plug for his hair-dryer. But he was a good, wee competitor and never pulled put of a tackle.

Birmingham was a big club. But The Blues should have done better and I always dreamed of playing in Europe with them one day. Even when we were struggling to avoid relegation, year after year, we were still getting average home gates of over 30,000. They are a sleeping giant and would get 40-50,000 every week if they were doing well.

It will be interesting to see what impact the new owner, Carson Yeung, has on the club. He has promised £80m for new players, but that's not enough in this day and age. You don't get much for £3m these days. There is already talk of a Champions League place – but that's Walt Disney talk. That's a million miles away.

Boss Alex McLeish needs to rebuild the promotion-winning team – and that's not going to happen overnight. I was in one or two squads with him over the years and he's an honest man. He's certainly got a big job on his hands, but he will do it – if he's allowed to do it his way. If not, he will walk away – as any decent manager would.

I never had a problem there at first, although I was always scrapping with big Joe Gallagher on the way to training. I hated training. I wasn't built for training. I didn't mind running with the ball – but running! I was the worst trainer in the history of the game.

We all got on well and several of us came through the youth team together. Our main duty was cleaning the terrace on the Spion Kop. We had to make sure the toilets and dressing rooms were clean and that all the training kit was loaded properly.

We used to pal about after training and when all the jobs were done, meet up for coffee, maybe have a game of snooker or go for a night out at the dogs – all on £8 a week wages.

One night this guy, who we didn't know from Adam, came up to me and Paul Hendrie at the dogs and gave us a winner. Very nice. In fact he gave us all seven that night and we went home with a cigar and about £60 each in our pocket – a tidy sum in those days.

Then there were the pubs and nightclubs, like the Rumrunner. I had never been to a nightclub and I have a lad called Stevie Phillips to thank for introducing me to them.

He knew the bouncers and got us in places like Barbarellas. Me in my flash velvet suit. He was the best man at my first wedding. He was also the man that led me astray. Not that I needed much leading.

He was my best pal, along with Jimmy Calderwood and Paul Hendrie, who was a hard, wee player.

Once Stevie persuaded me to go out to a party the night before a game against Arsenal Reserves. He said he had a couple of birds lined up.

Needless to say we ended up without any girls and getting blind drunk. I got pissed on Bacardi and coke, I've never felt so hung-over and I've never touched the stuff since. I moved on to vodka and lime but I like my beer these days and the occasional brandy – medicinal of course….

When it came to the match I was up against Welsh international John Roberts. He had a scything left foot that could cut an oak tree down. Just what I needed. I was awful and we lost 2-0.

Freddie Goodwin went mad. He ordered everyone in for extra training, apart from me – he thought I played well!

I had Ian Bolton, who went on to play for Notts County, Lincoln and Watford, to thank for getting me into betting. He took me into a bookies for my first bet and I won £4. That was me hooked. I liked a flutter on the ITV 7, but I was a mug punter, always trying to get back what I had lost the day before. At one time I'd bet on two flies going up a wall.

We got paid on a Friday and we had to do all our cleaning jobs to the satisfaction of kit man Ray Davey before catching a bus and dashing to the bank before it closed. We had about 15 minutes to get there, otherwise we wouldn't have any cash for the weekend.

One of my best memories from those early days was playing a youth team game against Aston Villa in front of a crowd of 12,000. We lost 1-0. I wasn't happy and chinned Bobby McDonald in the Oasis nightclub. He was a poser and was bragging about the result, so I chinned him. He deserved it.

But we had a cracking team with the likes of Gallagher, Phillips, keeper Paul Cooper and, of course, the Boy Wonder, Trevor Francis, who was already earning rave reviews. He would go on to score 133 goals in 328 games for the Blues. Trevor Francis became a god at Birmingham. He could do no wrong.

Francis had that rare commodity, pace, and the ability to get to the line at speed and cross accurately to the back post. He could run with the ball and he loved to score goals.

But he didn't clean boots, even though he was an apprentice, and that didn't sit to well with me. I cleaned Gary Pendry's boots and

Gordon Taylor's, I think. Was I jealous? Maybe.

But we came to an understanding in a five-a-side game. I whacked him and he suddenly stood up and got brave, so I had to give him a wee tap. We got on well after that; well well-ish!

I had some great digs at Alum Rock, which is like a war zone these days, with an old lady called Aunt Daisy. I was a skinny lad when I came down from Scotland, but she fed me up with roasts, and great chicken and vegetables. She was like a mum to me. She had a budgie. I hated the bloody thing and I kept opening the window, hoping it would fly away.

Poor Trevor had an old, bald landlady who served him fagots every night. That's one thing I didn't envy him.

One highlight for me was the 4-0 Youth Cup win over the Spurs youth team, who had Graeme Souness in their side, in front of over 13,000 at St Andrew's – and K Burns got two. Spurs were the holders but we swept into a 2-0 lead at the break. First I headed in a long cross from Lindley Jenkins in the 23rd minute. I had two defenders marking me, but timed my jump perfectly.

Then Trevor Francis forced his way to the bye-line and pulled a cross back for me to score with a diving header which went in off the far post. We rubbed it in with two goals in injury time from Steve Bryant and a Mike Harrison penalty.

I played left-half in five first-team matches but switched back to attack for the 2nd round of the FA Youth Cup against Northampton after the arrival of experienced Stan Harland.

Incredibly there was a crowd of 21,215 – more than some First Division attendances – for the 4th round tie with Villa on a cold, wet night at St Andrew's. It got a bit tasty, to say the least as the local rivalry boiled over and referee Harold Davey booked four players – three from Villa. They had future stars John Gidman, and Alan and Brian Little in their line-up, while we had Trevor Francis, Paul Cooper and Stevie Phillips, who had just made the breakthrough to the first team. I got away with a couple of bad challenges in the ankle-deep mud.

Villa opened the scoring in the 22nd minute when Tony Betts slid the ball past Cooper. It was the first goal we had conceded in the competition. Francis, who had begged manager Freddie Goodwin to let him play, was marked out of it by Jimmy Brown. But eight minutes into the second half he managed to escape his attentions. I headed his superb cross back and Steve Bryant did the business from three yards out.

I also scored in the FA Youth Cup quarter-final game at Arsenal. Trevor Francis had just earned rave reviews for scoring all four in the Division Two win over Bolton the previous Saturday, but we fell behind to goals from Paul Davis and Brian Hornsby in the last 20 minutes. I hit the bar and then got the consolation with three minutes to go. Russell Allen, who went on to play for Mansfield, was in the Arsenal side.

I wasn't so lucky in the Football Combination game at home to Southampton. I missed an open goal near the end and had a shot kicked off the line with the keeper beaten. We lost 1-0. But I bagged both goals in the 2-0 Combination win at Bournemouth. I tapped in the rebound after Tilsed, who was a youth international, parried a free-kick from Jenkins. Then, in the 53rd minute, I beat the keeper with a low, curling shot.

In 1971, I played at Stamford Bridge for the first time, in a 2-1 Combination win over Chelsea, who had big Droy at the back. We took the lead after only three minutes when Bowker calmly side footed in. With the last attack of the half the defence left a cross from Thwaites to each other, leaving me with a simple finish.

I picked up a few injuries but managed a goal for the Reserves against West Ham. Apart from Dave Latchford and Bobby Thompson, we were all teenagers. Stevie Phillips also scored twice, including the winner.

I had my first taste of European football, along with Joe O'Connor, Paul Cooper and Lindley Jenkins, in a four-team tournament in Basle where we won the Whitsun Youth tournament for the second successive year. We drew our first game 1-1 and then won 3-0. Then we beat Basle in the final and I got two of the goals. We were presented with a gold clock as a reward.

If that was an experience, so was getting married for the first time at 18, with a baby on the way. My wife, Pat, and me lived in a poxy flat above a shop on Ludlow Road. It wasn't great but it was all we could afford. We just had to get on with it. I had calmed down a little by now. The fact was that I couldn't afford to lose my temper any more.

But all that was to change one May day in 1972. I had been an automatic choice in Scotland's Professional Youth side and had apparently impressed manager Tommy Docherty in a trial match at Firhill.

I had just got home, after playing for Scotland in the Little World Cup in Spain, and a reporter was waiting for me at the flat. He said "phone this number, Tommy Docherty wants to talk to you." I thought it must be a wind up and checked in case it was April Fools Day. But I went out to the phone box, dialled the number and pressed button 'A' and The Doc answered the phone. He told me he wanted me to join up with the Scotland team at the training camp in Largs the following day.

I wasn't going to play, but he just wanted me to get a feel of things. He said that mixing with the likes of Law, Bremner and McNeill would do me the world of good. Me rubbing shoulders with Denis Law. I had to pinch myself to make sure I wasn't dreaming. After all, I had only played six first-team games for Birmingham at this stage.

I first met The Doc at Hull, who had an excellent player in Ken Wagstaff. I was getting ready to make my League debut as sub for Francis in 1971-72 when The Doc told me not to bother going on because I'd get my legs broken. Great. I was already crapping myself as it was. We lost 1-0.

I made my full debut, at the age of 17, in the 1-1 draw at Burnley. I played sweeper behind Roger Hynd in place of Dave Robinson. It was a bit of a shock but Goodwin had already given chances to Francis, Bowker, Harrison and Phillips. Nobody expected us to win because Burnley were in the middle of a tremendous run.

I got a nice introduction into life in Division Two when Frank Casper ran across me and gave me a fat lip. I waited for my chance to get revenge and, when the opportunity came, gave him a whack back. There was a bit of trouble and Roger Hynd pulled me out of the way.

Despite the fracas, I kept my place for the next seven games. I was only a kid but I didn't feel under any great pressure. I didn't feel out of my depth; I felt comfortable – until we played at Millwall. It was a horrible place to play and Derek Possee ran me ragged. Cocky as I was, I soon realised that I still had a lot to learn.

After that, I never got a look in after that as Bob Latchford hit 23 goals in 42 games to lead the club to promotion. Francis got 12 in 39 and Hatton 15 in 26. It was a remarkable achievement by Francis considering the amount of stick he took in matches. I take my hat off to him because referees actually allowed you to tackle in those days.

I thought, at the time, that sweeper was my best position. But, to be fair, I didn't mind where I played for Birmingham   up front, in defence of midfield – just as long as I was playing. I would even play in goal rather than not play at all.

The following season I was named as substitute for the first team and got my first League goal in the 3-2 defeat at Wolves. Despite scoring, I was back on the bench for the next game, a 4-1 home win over Manchester City, Latchford grabbing a hat-trick.

We then went on a bad run of only one win out of ten. I was sub against Newcastle (0-3), Derby (2-0) and Wolves (0-1). But I was finally given the No10 shirt for the last three home games of the season. We drew 0-0 with West Ham and I got the deciding goal in the 3-2 win over West Brom. Then Francis and me notched in the 2-1 win over Leeds as we finished 10th in Division One.

In 1973-74 Stan Harland had gone and I finally got a regular place in the side – if not a regular shirt. I started at No6 playing alongside Roger Hynd and also wore 4, 5, 7, 8, 9, 10, 11 and 12.

Roger was a great lad. He looked after me as we battled to beat the drop and I kept him touch with him over the years, although he's not in the best of health these days.

We could have done with Roger when we went on a tour to Belgium and Holland. Malcolm Page, Joe Gallagher, Gary Jones, Jimmy Calderwood, Peter Withe, Tony Want and myself went into a bar. I had a game of snooker with Gary, but it was a bit cramped and he tapped a young lady on the bum to ask her to move out of the way. Unfortunately, the man with her, a gypsy, took offence and a bit of a scuffle broke out. We all made a run for it but one of them tripped Peter Withe up and he broke his ankle.

Perhaps it was the gypsy curse, but we made a disastrous start to the season and didn't manage a win in the first ten games. I got a goal in the 2-2 draw at QPR and we finally managed a 2-1 home win over Wolves. Trevor Francis scored with a penalty and I got the other in front of a crowd of 34,977.

But it proved to be a false dawn and we lost to Manchester United, Everton and Stoke and drew 1-1 with Sheffield United and Southampton. Bob Latchford stopped the rot with a hat-trick in the 3-0 home win over Leicester and I got in on the act with the only goal against Newcastle and two in the 3-1 home win over West Ham.

One win in the next nine ensured that we were in for another season of struggle. But those remarkable fans didn't desert I us and there was an average home gate of 33,048.

My big break came when Freddie Goodwin pulled me to one side and asked if I fancied playing centre-forward at Wolves.

It was £25 extra if you played in the first team and I jumped at the chance. We lost 1-0, but I felt that I did ok. I must have been more than ok, because a few days later Bob Latchford, the local hero, was sold to Everton for £350,000. The rest, as they say, is history.

Bob had the ability to be one of the best centre-forwards England ever had and should have won more caps. He was big, strong as an ox and he had thighs like Popeye. Yes, he missed chances, but all good strikers do that.

Francis and myself scored in the 2-0 win at Southampton and I got my first hat-trick in the 3-3 draw at Leicester. Then I grabbed the winner in a vital 2-1 win over Norwich at St Andrew's after Stringer headed a superb goal in only the fourth minute. Bob Hatton equalised after 41 minutes after a good pass from Howard Kendall. I was foiled twice by keeper Keelan but, a minute before the break, Taylor swung over a cross from the left and I dived in to head my first goal at St Andrew's since the controversial sale of Bob Latchford.

With only one defeat in the last nine games we were safe and finished 19th in Division One. It was a great feeling to hear the happy crowd singing again.

We also had a good little run in the League Cup in the 1973-74 season. I scored in the 1-1 draw at Blackpool and we won the replay 4-2 with one from me and a Hatton hat-trick.

We beat Newcastle 1-0 after a replay and extra-time thanks to a Francis penalty and dumped Ipswich 3-1 with another Latchford hat-trick before going down 2-1 at home to Plymouth.

I had played several positions for the team, but I thought I was a good centre-forward after bagging ten goals in 36 League games. I believed I would always score goals. Why? Because I could jump higher than anyone else.

I had a teacher called Mr Ross to thank for that. He had me trying to head a swinging ball in the gym and taught me how to get my timing right. I also made a lot of goals for others. Say what you like about me, but I prided myself on being a team man.

Nothing phased me in those days. If I had been up against a John Terry or Rio Ferdinand, it wouldn't have bothered me. I knew that if I played to the best of my ability, it was them who would have problems with me.

I was on £35 a week then with £25 appearance money. When I became a regular in the first team it went up to £70 a week, which I didn't think was bad.

In 1974-75 our squad of 26 included eleven players who had come through from the youth team. Even Manchester United can't match that success rate. It was a remarkable achievement and I think it is one of the best squads Birmingham have ever had. Joe Gallagher had a tremendous attitude and his enthusiasm was second to none. Howard Kendall was a Rolls Royce in midfield and Bob Hatton was a deadly striker. Terry Hibbitt could almost make the ball talk. He could peel a grape with his feet.

That season we reached the semi-finals of the FA Cup and that was to lead to one of the biggest disappointments of my career...

The run started on January 4 with a 1-0 win at Luton. I scored in the 1-0 win at Chelsea and again in the 2-1 home win over Walsall. A goal from Hatton accounted for Middlesbrough to set up a last-four tie with Fulham at Hillsborough.

That was the tie we wanted because, even though they had the great Bobby Moore playing for them, they were a Second Division club. But we drew 1-1 with them and then lost the replay 1-0 after extra-time at Maine Road.

It was my saddest moment in football. It is no use moaning and looking back. It never changes anything, I know. But I never really did get over failing to get to the FA Cup Final at Wembley.

We again made a poor start to the League programme. I scored in the 4-3 home defeat by Leicester and the 1-1 draw with Wolves at St Andrew's. After five games without a win we finally got off the mark with a 1-0 victory at QPR with a goal from Gallagher.

Francis bagged two penalties in the 3-2 home win over Derby and I scored in the wins over Arsenal (3-1), Newcastle (3-0) and Manchester City (4-0).

But one win in eleven left us fighting for our lives again. I hadn't scored for 13 games but managed to sneak one in the 1-1 draw at Arsenal.

Home wins over QPR (4-1) and Carlisle (2-0) relieved some of the pressure, but we then messed up, losing four in a row.

But the 2-1 win over Newcastle and a 0-0 draw at home to Sheffield United ensured we finished 17th in Division One. I'd had a poor season by my standards with eight goals in 39 League games, but I'd also made goals for Francis (13) and Hatton (14).

The arrival of Peter Withe meant I was back in the No6 shirt for the 1975-76 season and I managed 36 league games. But although Francis hit 17, goals were at a premium with Withe and Hatton contributing only 17 between them. Fortunately, Howard Kendall got eight from midfield and I chipped in with five as we struggled to 19th in Division One.

Typically, we only took two points from the first seven games. We showed what we were capable of with a 4-0 win over Burnley, but leaked five against West Ham and Everton.

We had a squad of 21 for the 1976-77 season. Roberts, Hendrie, Hatton, Hope and Stevie Phillips had all gone and Withe played only three games before joining Forest.

So that was me back in the No9 shirt and I responded with 19 goals in 36 League games. I got off the mark in the first match – a 2-2 draw at Old Trafford in front of a massive crowd of nearly 59,000. I also scored in that very satisfying 2-1 win at Villa and the 1-2 defeat at Coventry. In the next match I famously got those four at home to Derby and kept the run going with goals against Middlesbrough (3-1), Bristol City (1-0) and QPR (2-1). We then went three games without a goal but bounced back to beat Leicester 6-2 with a K Burns treble.

Francis also got two hat-tricks that season as we contributed 40 goals between us. Mind you, five of his were penalties and I reckon he claimed one of mine. So, by my calculations we were level on 20 goals each.

I felt we had a good team. Unfortunately, everyone else had good sides in those days. It was no fun battling against relegation but I never, ever thought about leaving or asking for a transfer. I would have stayed there forever.

I suppose it all went sour for me at Birmingham when Goodwin was sacked and Willie Bell, who had played at Leeds, took over.

Now I got on well with Willie. He had made me skipper and even urged Willie Ormond to call me up to the Scotland team after I starred in the 1-0 win over Celtic and got man of the match in the 3-2 defeat at Coventry.

I got non-stop abuse from the crowd that day, after making a mistake that let David Cross in for a goal after 29 minutes. Then, on the stroke of half-time, Coventry's young Irish striker, Donald Murphy, was sent off for retaliation after taking a kick at me off the ball. I had a chance to make up for giving the goal away late on but I struck the ball too well. Maybe I should have dribbled round the keeper instead, the crowd would have loved that.

Bell turned against me when I ran into a bit of disciplinary trouble and got a four-match ban. To make matters worse it meant I also missed Scotland's U-23 European championship game with Holland.

Then, one day Bell suddenly dropped me. He told me he didn't fancy me at centre-half any more and was making me available for transfer.

I thought that was a bit harsh considering I usually started in defence and ended up front. After all I had scored 53 goals in 195 games, despite playing in a variety of positions.

Bell said I could train with the reserves if I liked, but it was close to the end of the season so I went on holiday. I was in Spain when I got a call from Bell telling me they had agreed a fee of £140,000 for me with Forest manager Brian Clough.

Bell was convinced I had been tapped up, but I had never spoken to Brian Clough in my life. I didn't even know I was on the list and wasn't aware of Forest's interest.

A couple of days later Cloughie called me and we arranged to meet at the Four Counties, a pub between Tamworth and Measham. I didn't know if I'd got enough petrol to get me there and was a bit worried because I hadn't got an MOT.

I tried to create a good impression by ordering half a lager and lime, as you do! Peter took me to one side for a quiet word. "Don't be too greedy, Ken when you go in there," he said. I can't remember what I asked for, but I finally came out of the pub agreeing to sign for £140 a week – more than double what I was on at Birmingham. They also offered me £14,000 cash, in two instalments (I think I got it in about 150). Where do I sign?

"Get your hair cut Kenneth," was BC's parting shot as we agreed to meet again the following day at another pub, the Derbyshire Yeoman. Cloughie took my wife and me to a sweet pea show at Bramcote. This was something new to me, because the only peas I'd ever seen were of the mushy variety.

I was later told that Peter had been following me about at the Perry Bar dog track to see what kind of character I was.

I never did get my hair cut. I never had the time......pre-season started the following day.

Above: The superb Birmingham youth team. Back: Joe Gallagher, Trevor Francis, Dave Howitt, Paul Cooper, Mike England, Steve Bryant, Mick Morris. Middle: Gary Emannuel, Terry Shipman, Stevie Phillips, Ray Davey, Joe Connor, Len Jenkins, Bobby Fryer. Front: K Burns and Bobby Goode. Left: Scoring in Basle on my first European tour. Below: The teams line up before the start of the tournament

Birmingham squad 1975

Celebrating with the fans

Celebrating being named Midland Player of the Year with Trevor Francis, John Roberts and Gary Sprake

My trademark flowing locks!

FOUR-GOAL KEN

Blues five! — Albion m four

BLUES v DERBY.

KENNY Burns is the toast of Birmingham City after a sensational show of fire-power which pole-axed Derby at St. Andrew's.

The super Scot smashed four goals as scintilating Blues crushed out-of-touch Derby.

Three of his goals came before half-time, and his magnificent performance might have contained two more

---

OTHER N FOR URNS

NNY BURNS, e Birmingham er who starts a -match ban this end, learned rday he must a fourth.

tland manager Ormond asked for release for the r-22 European pionship game Holland on March

Willie Bell, Bir- ham's Scots-born said: "I had to hems Kenny's sus- ion prevents it.

Future

his is an added shment for a club been a good inter- nal opportunity for

Burns knows this h

---

urns switches to striker for Blues Youth Cup clash

Main Sports Reporter

TEENAGER Ken Burns was today named to lead the Birmingham City youth team attack at St. Andrew's tomorrow night after playing at left-half in the last five first team matches.

A.T.V. (tomorrow 2.10):

Burn's switch from defen- sive stopper to striker comes in the second rou F.A. Youth Cup m t Northampton Blues Manager Goodwin, explainin said today: "Burn as a defensive play we switched him forward position fo

"He did exception this role and I be him as an extre de striker. In fact mendous scoring pe he played i, because of t lem in the first te to give Burns a the back four.

'Good

"But now I see h as a striker and ' role again to th is no reflection has done a good I feel we ar have a young p who has the qual

---

FOOTBALL COMBINATION

Burns steps in with fine 1-2

Bournemouth 0, Birmingham 2

THE greater experience of Birmingham Reserves stood them in good stead against the young Bournemouth side.

Although the Hampshire team saw rather more of the ball, especially in the early stages, their attacks lacked bite against a resolute defence.

Birmingham's first goal was a "gift" from Bournemouth's youth international keeper.

The keeper, taking the return from a goal kick, strayed outside his area, before throwing the ball up field.

Jenkins' resultant free kick was well barried but the ball ran loose and Burns had the simplest of tasks to net.

Skipper Bobby Thomson set up the movement through which Burns made it 2-0 in the 33rd minute. The centre forward's low

---

SUPERB KEN SIZZLES TO HAT-TRICK

by DENNIS SHAW

Leicester 3, Blues 3

LUES fought back from 2-0 down to 3-2 up before being pegged at 3-3 midway through nd-half as Kenny Burns scored a spec at-trick against Leicester at Filber

ond minute goal Cross Blues -0 as Len Glover ond in the 19th

e game seemingly ruck after 21, 40, to turn the game

equalised after

Y: Shilton; Whit- rle, Munro, Cross, eis, Worthington. Sub.: Partridge. TTY: Latchford; , Kendall, Hynd, pbell, Francis, Taylor. Sub.:

Park Rangers and Nor- wch.

was well placed but it must been a hairline decision!

There was tremendous char about the way Blues continu force their way into attack pace and mobility of Burn causing Cross all sorts of in the centre of the Le defence.

One ball he won in the a a left-wing cross by Tayl deflected for a corner defender.

A similar move seconds the 48th minute, enabled who has filled in so well Latchford, to thump a n equaliser.

Once again BURNS had his to go past Cross it pursuit of an angled through-ball from Campbell out on the left.

Burns chased it, veering to the right and judging the bounce When

---

THE SUNDAY POST, DECEMBER

KENNY'S GOAL IS WORTH £3000!

SCOTLAND World Cup man KENNY BURNS turned down a gift of a sports car yesterday — for the good of his Birmingham team-mates.

Kenny, you see, was entitled to the car as a prize offered by a local garage owner to any City player who scored his side's sixth goal in ANY game.

Well, Kenny did just that yesterday an Birmingham's six goal r out at Leicester, but after the game he turned down his prize. Reason? He opted instead the cash value, £3000, shares with the

Birmingham almost won the car on October 3 when they beat Derby 5-1, with Burns notching four on that occasion.

It was felt at the time the prize of the car could cause an untidy stampede to grab that all- goal. But that

DAILY RECORD, Tuesday, January 18, 1977

It's crisis time for Ken Burns

KENNY BURNS, Birmingham City's 23-year- old Scottish international, was warned yesterday that he is at the crossroads of his career.

Willie Bell, the manager who put him on the transfer list a week ago, said: "I haven't had one inquiry for him.

"Kenny is a current Scottish international, a player of tremendous ability and one of the leading scorers in the country. But it seems nobody wants to buy him. He must ask himself if that is Birming

must cularly he has es for reasons!

URNS HOPES BURN BRIGHT

By HUGH JAMIESON

GHAM, happy at the prospect of three out of four games at home, hope to have striker Kenny for tomorrow night's visit of Burnley.

who damaged his achilles tendon in the Good Friday Burnley, has been under intensive treatment while 19- defender Joe Gallagher has taken over in an emergency

I never had time for a hair cut

Forest Fire
(1977-1978)

I used to travel up from Sutton Coldfield, but the boss wanted me to move closer to Nottingham. I ended up renting a property in East Leake, then I moved to Toton, which was nice.

I like my snooker –I've got a best break of 51 – and I used to play a frame or two at the Copsey Croft pub near the old Long Eaton speedway stadium with a mate of mine called John Burns. Sadly, I think it's gone now.

I used to put the dog, a rough collie, over the fence, and walk it across the fields. But it was never the same when we got it back from the kennels one year, it was crapping all over the house, and my wife made me get rid of it. I loved that dog. It broke my heart to see it go.

I should have kept the dog and got rid of the wife.

When we started to get a wee bit of success I got a place in Clifton Village.

Just after I signed for Forest we went away for ten days pre-season to West Germany, Austria and Switzerland. We had five practice matches fixed up and the boys assumed I would be centre-forward after scoring 20 goals the previous season with Birmingham. Peter Withe and Tony Woodcock thought they might be the ones to miss out, but Clough and Taylor obviously had other ideas. They wanted me to replace Sammy Chapman.

In the absence of Clough & Taylor (they were nowhere to be seen), trainer Jimmy Gordon read out the team and I was playing at the back with Larry Lloyd against St Gallen. No-one had said anything to me. And I never asked.

I was just happy to be playing football again. I was a bit overweight when I joined Forest. I ate too much of the wrong food and drank quite a bit, too. But, under Clough & Taylor I soon got my enthusiasm for the game back.

I had an incentive to do well again and cut down on the food and drink. I used to wear bin liners under my top to help work up a sweat until I got down to my 'fighting' weight – 13 stone.

Of course I missed scoring goals, but it didn't bother me. Anyway, there was less running to do at the back.

We won the first game 3-2 with two goals from Withe and one from Ian Bowyer.

Apart from me, the team was pretty much the one that had gained promotion. John Middleton was in goal. A big lad, he looked the part, but he soon made way for Peter Shilton as part of the deal that brought Archie Gemmill from Derby. The boss had obviously spotted some flaws in him. Viv Anderson and Colin Barrett were the full-backs with John McGovern and Ian Bowyer holding midfield and Curran, O'Neill, Woodcock, Withe and Robertson always likely to get you a goal.

When I made my debut there were no tactics mentioned; we just went out and played.

I was in the team for the wins against Wacker Innsbruck (2-0) and SV Platting (5-1) but the match with Insbruck got a bit tasty and Peter Withe, who had his nose broken, got sent off for retaliation.

He was apparently sent home by Clough as a disciplinary measure, but it conveniently allowed him to get treatment and he had also just become a father for the second time, so you can draw your own conclusions.

I was rested for the game against Neuburg, which we won 5-1. Me and Terry Curran went drinking and sat in the sunshine to pass the time. That night we went to a Bier Keller and I was well out of it after playing a drinking game with the lads. I almost spilled a drink over Mrs Clough before Larry and the lads dragged me out.

At least I made it to breakfast. When the gaffer came in I asked if I could have a word and apologised for my behaviour the night before. "It's a good job you came to see me because you were on the next plane home," said the boss

I think we won the last game, against SW Bregnez, 3-0, before flying back to play, would you believe, Skegness, in a friendly. We got a magnum of champagne each for that one.

I got a goal in the 4-0 win which turned out to be Terry Curran's last game for the club, as he made way for the hard-working Martin O'Neill. Then we drew 1-1 with Notts County in the County Cup, winning on penalties. They had a cracking team then and in Jimmy Sirrel had one of the most knowledgeable men in football. He knew everybody and I regret that I never got to know him better before he died.

Suddenly the season was upon us and the gaffer decided to leave Curran out, replacing him with O'Neill. We made a great start with a 3-1 win at Everton – I thought we played superbly that day.

Then we beat Bristol City, Derby County and West Ham without conceding a goal. We did Derby 3-0 with two from Withe and one from Robertson and, although it was a local derby, it didn't mean that much to me. I didn't know much about the rivalry between the two clubs and it didn't seem to have the same passion as Birmingham v Villa.

At the end of the day we were top of the league, the only team with maximum points from three games.

With confidence high we whipped West Ham 5-0 in the League Cup, but we came back down to earth at Highbury when we lost 3-0 to Arsenal.

There were a couple of incidents in the match and afterwards Cloughie fined me and Larry. To make matters worse we lost Clark with a hamstring injury. I was caught sticking the nut on Richie Powling at a free-kick. I didn't think anyone was looking – apart from the 40,000 in Highbury that day of course. The ref and linesman didn't see anything but what I didn't realise was that a television camera was trained on me at the time.

I sat at home watching t.v. with my dinner on my knee when the incident came on. I shot up in the air and the dinner ended up on the floor.

I thought I was for the high-jump, but nothing was said at training. Then Jimmy Gordon came in and said there was a players' meeting in the committee room. Cloughie came in and handed me an envelope with a red tree on it. Inside was a fine for £50. He never said a word. I thought "I'll take that" and that was the end of it.

Meanwhile, Cloughie offered Stoke £270,000 for Peter Shilton, which was a hell of a lot of money for a goalkeeper in those days. He made his debut in the home game with Villa, which we comfortably won 2-0 through Robertson and Woodcock, who was starting to look the part up front. Shilts turned out to be some signing. He only conceded 17 goals in Division One that season. Truly world class.

There was another shock in store for us when Archie Gemmill – the final piece in Clough & Taylor's jig-saw – arrived from Derby, with John Middleton and Terry Curran moving in the opposite direction. It also spelt the end for Sean Haslegrave, who went to Preston.

I got my first League goal for the club in the 1-1 home draw with Norwich. Cloughie wasn't happy about conceding our first League goal at home, after five clean sheets, and dropped Archie for the game with Ipswich. I remember we beat an Ipswich side laced with internationals, 4-0. That was very satisfying because Mick Mills had said before the game that we were a team of has-beens. Pete Withe, who would run all day for you, got three, but BC wouldn't give him the match ball at first. "You can have the ball when you learn to play with it properly," he said. He made him sweat for a couple of days before he gave it to him.

In another game, against Ipswich, Peter flicked the ball on a couple of times early on and the gaffer went mad and pulled him off. The referee came over and told him to bring the sub on but BC just said "Carry on." He played the rest of the game with ten men just to teach us a lesson. All he wanted the centre-forward to do was two things - hold the ball up and stick it in the net. Cloughie gave you a job to do and if you didn't do it you were out. Simple as that!

Every game was a cup final for me. I was desperate to keep a clean sheet. It was like a badge of honour. That's the way I played. I always played to win. The opposition was like the enemy to me – even if I was playing against my best pal.

We kept another clean sheet at West Ham and there were 35,572 at the City Ground to see us beat Manchester City 2-1 through Withe and Woodcock. I notched in the 2-0 win at QPR and we then beat

Notts County 4-0 in the League Cup to emphasise the growing gulf between the two clubs. Four days later we put four past Middlesbrough. We went top of the league after nine games and that's where we stayed – despite losing 1-0 at Chelsea. I even managed another goal, in the 2-1 win over Manchester United.

We lost 1-0 in a cracker at Leeds which must have hurt the gaffer after the way he had been treated there. But it was the last League game we lost all season. Cloughie's answer to the defeat was a mid-week trip to Israel to play a friendly with Maccabi Tel Aviv. We won 6-1, with sub John O'Hare bagging one of the goals.

We drew Villa at home in the League Cup and won 4-2. Cloughie thought about dropping Withe, who had drawn a few blanks after grabbing about ten in ten, but he scored. Then Shilts, who had been cup-tied for the Villa game, played a blinder as we beat Birmingham 2-0 away, denying my mate Francis a goal in the process.

Unfortunately, Larry Lloyd broke a bone in his foot in the 2-1 win over Coventry so in came former Notts County favourite David Needham from QPR (the following day), which didn't sit too well with Larry.

Needham was thrown in for his debut against Manchester United at Old Trafford. Woodcock got two as we strolled to a 4-0 win in front of over 54,000. To be fair, we could have eight that day. We were that good.

As a reward we went off to Spain for a team-bonding break in the sun, coming back for the Boxing Day 1-1 draw against Liverpool at the City Ground. Archie Gemmill got the goal. We ended the year on a high with a 2-0 win at Newcastle and a 3-1 success at Bristol City.

Forest started 1978 with a 1-1 home draw with Everton, Robbo scoring from the spot, and eased past Swindon 4-1 and Manchester City 2-1 in the FA Cup and Bury 3-0 in the fifth round of the League Cup. Suddenly, we found ourselves chasing the treble after beating Leeds 7-3 on aggregate in the semi-finals of the League Cup and dumping QPR, at the third time of asking, in the FA Cup.

Amazingly Cloughie was away on a family holiday in Spain while all this was happening but he cut it short for the QPR replay, which we won 3-1, thanks to goals from the impressive O'Neill and Woodcock (2). Our resources were stretched to the limit with injuries and suspensions and our unbeaten run of 22 games ended when we lost 2-0 at West Brom in the FA Cup. Big Cyrille Regis, who had been snapped up from local football after being rejected by Chelsea as a youngster, got one of the goals.

It wasn't the best preparation for the League Cup final with Liverpool, especially as we would be without Shilton, Needham, Gemmill and Barrett.

We spent the night at the Hendon Hall Hotel and were amazed how many fans had made the trip to Wembley to cheer us on. There was a crowd of 100,000 in there that day.

Brian wanted Peter to lead the team out with him, but the powers that be wouldn't let him. It was a great feeling walking out at Wembley and soaking up the atmosphere. The Bernabeau was special, it was a crime to walk on the pitch, it was so beautiful. But Hampden Park was better; the crowd would lift the roof off. The supporters at the Rangers end would be trying to out-sing the Celtic side. Forget the Welsh, if you want to hear passionate singing go to a Scotland match. It makes the hair on the back of your neck stand on end. To be fair, we were under a lot of pressure but 18-year-old Chris Woods, who had never even played a league match remember, was superb as we drew 0-0 after extra-time.

Larry was also immense against his old club who should probably have won to be fair. Terry McDermott had the ball in the net, but Kenny Dalglish had just crept off-side.

No-one really wanted the replay at Old Trafford on the Wednesday night, especially as McGovern, who had aggravated his groin injury, had no chance of playing. John O'Hare took his place in midfield and earned the penalty that won the game when Phil Thompson brought him down from behind. It was a controversial decision but I reckon John's finger-nails were in the area – just. Fortunately, referee Pat Partridge agreed and Robbo tucked away the penalty, as usual. McDermott again had a goal disallowed, this time for hands, but we had the best of the chances in the second half.

I was the first person to lift the League Cup. Larry had taken it upon himself to be skipper. But the boss threw the ball to me in the replay and told me to lead them out. Big Larry wasn't happy with that, but he was always at loggerheads with the gaffer anyway.

When I lifted the Cup it was one of the greatest moments of my life. I couldn't wait to get my hands on the trophy and do the lap of honour. But I was sorry for John because it deserved to be him.

Winning the cup guaranteed Forest a place in the UEFA Cup. But that wasn't good enough for Clough & Taylor – they wanted European Cup glory.

We only needed six points from eight games to take the title, but it didn't stop the gaffer putting out a full-strength side in a testimonial for Notts County favourite Les Bradd. A crowd of over 10,000 saw us win 1-0 with a 69th-minute goal from John O'Hare. Sammy Chapman and Tristan Benjamin were outstanding at the back for County, while Shilts made a world-class save from Arthur Mann, sadly no longer with us. The goal came when Eric McManus parried a shot from Ian Bowyer. I knocked it back across goal and O'Hare did the rest.

We clinched the title, with four games left to play, with a 0-0 draw at Coventry. We were presented with the trophy in the final home game of the season, ironically against my old club Birmingham, who held us to a 0-0 draw. No matter, that result meant we had created a club record of 23 games unbeaten at home.

I played 68 games in all that season but I missed the final match, a 0-0 draw against Liverpool, to collect the sports writer's Player of the Year award from comedian Billy Connolly. I also won Midland Player of the Year. I think we swept the board. Shilts was PFA Player of the Year, Tony Woodcock was Young Player of the Year and Cloughie was, of course, Manager of the Year.

That first season was a dream. I think we only lost four games out of 70. You know, John Robertson only missed one of those – and that was a pre-season friendly. It was staggering how many clean sheets we kept. And we didn't just hump the ball. We played passing football all the way. It was a special team – and I am proud to have been part of it all.

Happy days.

Me in action against Leeds' Frank and Eddie Gray and Paul Madeley

I wave to the fans before the League Cup Final against Liverpool at Wembley

Celebrating winning the 1979 League Cup final

We show off the League Championship Trophy before the home game with Birmingham

I wind down with a drink or two with Peter Withe and John McGovern

Midlands Sports Writers Player of the Year

Kings of Europe
(1978-1979)

I got back from Argentina determined to wipe away the disappointment of the World Cup campaign with Scotland, but suddenly found myself packing again for a pre-season tour of Yugoslavia and Greece.

We had some tough games and got beat 3-2 by Red Star Belgrade with the usual suspects – Shilton, Anderson, Barrett, McGovern, Lloyd, Burns, O'Neill, Gemmill, Withe, Woodcock and Robertson. We drew the other three, against Dynamo Zagreb, SK Osijek and AKE Athens, 1-1. The games were more like cup ties than pre-season friendlies. We had to come back for the pre-season curtain raiser, the Charity Shield game against Ipswich, so at least they were a good preparation. I think!

Cloughie wanted Peter Taylor to lead the team out but, again, his request was turned down. We played with a horrible red and white ball and the pitch was quite heavy, but we performed exceptionally well against a good side.

I was chuffed for Colin Barrett who had finally made it to Wembley and even happier after the match, which we won 5-0. Can you believe that? They were certainly no mugs and had my old Birmingham team-mate Paul Cooper in goal. Martin O'Neill had scored two, but Cloughie wasn't happy. He wanted him to pass more and, even though he was on a hat-trick, the boss pulled him off after what he thought was a bit of poor control.

Withe got one, Lloyd scored a minute after the break and Robbo capped a great display with the last two minutes from time.

We didn't have too much time to bask in the glory of the Wembley win because we were off to Spain for games against Celta Vigo (1-1) and FC Porto (0-1).

Three days later we kicked off with a 1-1 home draw with Spurs, who had signed Argentine stars Ricardo Villa and Ossie Ardiles for a joint fee of £750,000 in the close season. There was a big buzz around because those two were playing. They were the first foreigners to make a real impression on the English game and proved to be inspired signings by Keith Burkinshaw. They were quality players and quality players can fit in anywhere in the world.

So many turned up that the gates had to be closed well before kick-off. Martin O'Neill gave us the lead before Villa capped his debut with the equaliser.

After the match we found out that Pete Withe, who was coming to the end of his contract, had asked for a transfer. The story was that he only wanted a £25 pay rise but the boss wouldn't give it him. I think Pete really wanted to stay, but there was no turning back now and before we knew it he was off to Newcastle for £250,000. I had played with Withe at Birmingham and was certainly sorry to see him go. He would chase all day and turn a bad ball into a good one.

Although we had players all over the park capable of scoring goals, I felt it left us very short up front, but the boss thought he had a ready-made replacement in young Steve Elliott.

Now Cloughie thought highly of Elliott, who had big shoulders like John O'Hare. Unfortunately, he didn't play anything like O'Hare. He struggled with injuries and never quite made it. The next four games were all 0-0 draws, which was unusual for us. Tony Woodcock, for one, desperately needed the boost of a goal after going nine games without hitting the net.

So I took it upon myself to remind him how it was done in the League Cup against Oldham. We also put six past Mansfield in a friendly but the gaffer wasn't satisfied and decided to gamble on Garry Birtles, a former carpet fitter from Long Eaton who had been getting a few goals for the reserves, and 16-year-old Gary Mills, for the home game with Arsenal.

It was a big ask of the fresh-faced Birtles. There was nothing on him. But he went on to become one of the best all-round strikers in the country. We got our first League win of the season, 2-1 through Bowyer and Robertson, and never really looked back.

Next up was the first round of the European Cup. We wanted a European giant, a Real Madrid or a Benfica, a nice little trip abroad.

And who did we get at the draw in Zurich? Defending champions Liverpool! I couldn't believe it. Birtles, who had worked hard against the Gunners, deservedly kept his place and was an instant hero in the thrilling 2-0 win. I had a hand in the first goal with a chip over Graeme Souness. Woodcock squared the ball and Birtles tapped in his first goal for the club. It looked like that would be it, but with time running out Colin Barrett won the ball and released Birtles. He beat Phil Thompson and his cross was headed down by Woodcock to the rampaging Barrett, who volleyed in from six yards. The Liverpool dressing-room wasn't a happy place after the game, I can tell you.

Sadly, Barrett tore knee ligaments in the 2-2 draw at Middlesbrough and faced a long spell on the sidelines. He was never the same player again, which was a shame because he was a nice lad and he never let you down.

The Liverpool result didn't surprise me. In four games against us they hadn't scored a goal, while we put four past them.

We stayed at a hotel near Liverpool before the second leg of the Cup and the boss ordered a few bottles of wine to make sure we got a good kip that afternoon.

We needed it because it was backs-to-the-wall in the return at Anfield as they came at us in waves. They got desperate when it came to the last 15 minutes and just lumped it forward, which suited me and Larry down to the ground. They got a bit frustrated and Kenny Dalglish, of all people, caught me with a late tackle. Unusually for me, I didn't react. It was a disciplined performance.

In fact, if one word summed up our play it was DISCIPLINE.

Frank Clark, who had considered quitting to become a coach, came in for his first game of the season for the unfortunate Barrett. Frank had a gash in his shin stitched up at half-time but, typically, he never let it bother him as we held on for a famous 0-0 draw.

We had AEK Athens in the 2nd round. We had played a friendly there and knew they had a few Greek internationals in the side and were managed by the great Ferenc Puskas, but that was about it.

We went 1-0 up with a scrambled goal after a quick free-kick from Frank Clark, who then ran half the field to set up Birtles for the second. The turning point came when Milton Viera punched me in the face and got sent off. I got booked for my part in the incident. The crowd got a bit frisky after that and I think the referee was looking to even things up when he gave a harsh penalty against me to make it 2-1. It wasn't a foul ... trust me.

But the most publicised incident came as we left the hotel to fly home. The boss had ordered everyone to smarten up for the trip and to come down in a tie and club blazer. Everyone did, except big Larry, who was dressed casually in jeans and a shirt.

Cloughie told him to go and get changed but Larry said his stuff was packed at the bottom of his suitcase, which was on the coach. The gaffer said he had time because we were going to have a glass of champagne before we left, but Larry didn't bother.

When we flew back we were staying at the old Midland Hotel opposite the railway station in Derby and the coach came to take us to training at the City Ground. After training we were called to a meeting in the committee room. The gaffer gave Larry the dreaded envelope – fined £100 for breach of club discipline. Larry argued and Cloughie added £100 every time he opened his mouth "Another thing," said Clough: "You're not playing tomorrow."

As a parting shot the gaffer said he was a better player than Larry would ever be. "Yes, in the Second Division," replied Larry, quick as a shot. The big man went off in a huff and asked for a transfer. Larry insists to this day that he was never told to wear club uniform. I think Larry withdrew his transfer request after a showdown with Peter Taylor and ended up just paying the £100.

Cloughie flew out for a break in the sun with his family but was back in the time for the return leg with the Greeks. I was suspended so David Needham came in and Cloughie, typically, named Larry as skipper. Needham gave us the lead with a header and it was one-way traffic after that as we won 5-1.

The next cup match was in the League Cup at Everton and it's a game I will never forget because I picked up my first serious injury. I heard something in my knee crack and knew I had done some damage. Jimmy Gordon managed to click it back in and at half-time I had an injection in my arse. As I went out for the second half the gaffer said: "Kenneth, don't let them see you limping." I thought: 'Thanks very much for your sympathy.'

I had an operation at Harlow Wood and missed about a dozen games, but at least I had Colin Barrett for company in rehab. Brian Clough called to ask if I needed anything and I said "Yes, get me out of here." I was in for about five days and it was driving me mad. I was bored to tears but they said I couldn't leave until I was able to lift my leg off the bed.

I came back for the FA Cup game with York at the end of January, which we won 4-1 and then played in the 2nd leg of the League Cup semi-final with Watford, who caused us more than a few problems before we won 3-1 on aggregate. But then I injured my calf and faced an even longer spell on the sidelines.

I hated being injured. But I suppose I had been very lucky over the years. I was always getting hit in the mouth and had a major bridge job. I actually knocked two teeth out myself with a mobile phone, believe it or not.

But the worst came when I fell off a horse, while I was with Birmingham. Yes, a horse. It happened when I was on holiday near Bournemouth in June 1979. My wife talked me into going horse riding but I wasn't too keen. She went on until I agreed and I did ok at first. But then the bloody thing bolted while I only had one foot in the stirrup and I got dragged along. I bashed my back and my wrist and, as a result, had to pull out of the Scotland squad for their tour of South America.

On this occasion I missed the 1-0 FA Cup defeat by Arsenal, the League Cup final against Southampton, which we won 3-2, the two European games against Grasshoppers Zurich and the first-leg draw with Cologne. But David Needham did a great job in my absence.

While I was on the sidelines the £1m-man – give a penny or two – got into the side and he notched his first goal to salvage a point in a 1-1 draw with Bolton.

I hated being injured, there is nothing worse, and I finally came back in the 2-1 win at Derby in place of Larry. But Colin Barrett's knee had gone again and he was back in hospital.

We had been held 3-3 in the home leg by Cologne, who had

decided attack was the best policy. They went 2-0 up before Birtles and Bowyer pulled us level. Robbo gave us the lead with a rare diving header, but we were sunk by a Japanese sub Yasuhiko Okudera, who had only been on the pitch for about a minute, after a rare mistake by Shilts.

Everybody was writing us off – apart from Peter Taylor. "Get your heads up we will win this one. We can win this," he kept insisting. I think he must have had a few quid on at the bookies.

We didn't train much before the match, we sat round relaxing, drinking, playing cards – the usual. When we got to the stadium, I didn't like it. It had a running track round it and you all know how I feel about running. The plan was to keep a clean sheet and perhaps snatch a late winner. Muller, their centre-forward, had been saying the match was all over. Well, it was all over for him after about 30 minutes. Me and Larry soon sorted him out.

As it happens the plan worked a treat and we got the crucial goal in the 64th minute when Ian Bowyer, who was next to me, stooped to head in a corner from Robbo. Shilts made a good late save and we were in the final of the European Cup. It was Roy of the Rovers stuff, something every kid dreams of.

Three days after that we were in action at home to Liverpool (0-0) but we had good home wins over Southampton and Man City before beating Leeds 2-1 and West Brom 1-0 away. A goal from Trevor Francis in the 81st minute was enough to clinch second spot – albeit eight points behind Liverpool. The last game before the European Cup final was the County Cup final against Mansfield. The Stags actually took the lead through Russ Allen, but Francis inspired a fight back with Lloyd and Robbo getting the others.

The European Cup final, against injury-hit Malmo, wasn't much better. It was a bit of a damp squib despite a crowd of 80,000 in the Olympic Stadium in Munich. It was a bit boring to be truthful. No-one had heard of little Malmo, who were coached by an Englishman called Bobby Houghton. And, to be fair, although they were well organised, they were a poor side.

We won 1-0 thanks to a bit of magic from Robbo, but it was Trevor Francis who grabbed the headlines with the far-post headed goal just before half-time. Cloughie decided to go with Francis after picking Frank Clark ahead of Martin O'Neill and Archie Gemmill.

He asked them if they were both fit and they said "Yes." Cloughie said "I'm pleased for you both; you're on the bench." Archie says the gaffer promised him that he would be playing. He was furious. I don't think he ever forgave Cloughie and he had a blazing row. He picked the wrong time for a public fight and it probably led to him leaving for Birmingham, even though he had a year left on his contract. I made a couple of uncharacteristic mistakes in the game but got away with them after Larry covered my back.

We had won the European Cup but the mood in the dressing room was a bit flat. We had wanted to win it in style. After the match Cloughie said he wanted all the medals so he could have copies made and Archie threw his on the floor. He never played for Forest again.

We didn't even celebrate much that night but, when we got back to Nottingham, an estimated 200,000 people turned out to see the cup paraded on an open-topped bus.

The bus went all over the place and everywhere we went the people were four or five deep on both sides of the road. It was a magnificent sight.

It was a great moment when I lifted the European Cup for the first time. I thought back to its history; all the great players that had touched it. I never get tired of looking at that picture.

We finished runners-up in the League behind Liverpool that season after playing seven games in 21 days. Gallingly, we only lost three League games all season, while Liverpool lost four.

That season, we had played 76 games, and you know what? Robbo appeared in every one of them, including friendlies and testimonials - although the boss always insisted there was no such thing as a friendly.

When we played in a testimonial at Sheffield United it was 0-0 at half-time. We didn't realise the gaffer was there and he went ape-shit in the dressing room. He absolutely slaughtered us and we went back out and won 6-1. We didn't mind testimonials and friendlies because we usually had a good social afterwards and, you know me, I would always rather play than train.

Charity Shield against Ipswich. We won 5-0

Garry Birtles scores in the League Cup Final against Southampton

Warming up for the European Cup Final against Malmo

Champions of Europe, but Malmo were a poor side

Me and Bomber with the cup

Showing off the cup back home in Nottingham. Below: The kings of Europe

You have to be prepared to put your head in where it hurts

Back to back
(1979-1980)

As usual we had a busy pre-season with games in Denmark, West Germany, Spain and France. But it was better than training. We started with a match against Holsterbro BK, which we won 5-1 in front of about 3,000 fans. Martin O'Neill was the star, grabbing a hat-trick, after deciding he didn't want to leave the City Ground after all. I got one as well before making way for David Needham.

But it was to be the last game Colin Barrett played because of his knee injuries. His replacement, Frank Gray, came in for his debut against Bayern Munich and must have wondered what he had let himself in for as they hammered us 5-0.

It wasn't a happy return to the Olympic Stadium and nobody played well that day. It started badly for me when I scored an own goal and it just went from bad to worse. We were lacking match fitness, while they were flying and boasted players like Niedermayer, Paul Breitner and Dieter Hoeness.

But 5-0 was still a bad result. Let's be honest, they gave us a right spanking.

Asa Hartford, a busy little player but not that special, was in for Archie. Mr Angry had been told in no uncertain terms by Peter Taylor that he had no future at the club and was shipped off to Birmingham for £150,000. But there was no sign of my mate Trevor Francis, who had apparently got himself fixed up in America. He'd got himself a nice little £50,000 deal to play for Detroit Express for two seasons. And, to be fair, he did well with 36 goals in 33 games.

Botafogo kicked lumps off us in what was supposed to be a "prestige" tournament in Spain, but the ref kept giving them the free-kicks. They were animals and the crowd were pelting us with bricks and bottles. For the next 45 minutes we just played keep-ball and kept out of harm's way to win 2-1. Shilts had a great game, the goals coming from Birtles and Woodcock.

Then Robbo got both goals as we beat Romanian side Dinamo Bucharest 2-1 in the final. Robbo was brilliant that night. His first was a rare header and he also tucked away a penalty after Woodcock was brought down.

We rounded things off in France with a 1-0 win over Montpellier thanks to another Robbo spot-kick. To be honest, for once, I was glad to get back home to the wife.

We carried on where we left off in the League with 1-0 wins over Ipswich and Stoke, although I was banned after picking up 20 disciplinary points.

We beat Coventry 4-1 with a couple of John McGovern goals, which are as rare as hen's teeth. Then Cloughie dropped a bombshell, even by his own high standards, when he sold Hartford to Everton, at a loss, after just 63 days at the club. He admitted that he had made a mistake and there was talk that he'd even tried to get Archie Gemmill back from Birmingham, but Archie wasn't having any of it.

But the goals were starting to flow now. We beat Blackburn 7-2 on aggregate in the League Cup and Garry Birtles got a hat-trick as we put five past a very good West Brom side, away, after going one down after about a minute. I thought I had scored a cracker that day, right into the top corner, but the ref blew for half-time while the ball was in the air. Typical of my luck with referees.

We needed to carry that type of form into the first leg of the European Cup tie with Osters Vaxjo, but we drew 0-0 with Leeds and lost 3-1 at Norwich.

I hit a post against the Swedes before Ian Bowyer bagged two. Job done. We were back on course and beat Middlesbrough 3-1 away in the League Cup with a hat-trick from Woodcock. Could we make it an incredible three in a row? Sadly, the answer was no.

We drew the second leg with Osters 1-1 with a late goal from Woodcock, although, to be honest, I don't remember too much about the game. Francis was back from America where he had been playing for Detroit – but he had come back injured and didn't kick a ball for us until October 6 when we beat Wolves 3-1. Typically, old golden bollocks announced his return with a goal after just a few seconds.

We'd drawn a Romanian side, Arges Pitesti in the next round of the European Cup. I'd never heard of them, but they had beaten AEK Athens to get this far so they couldn't be mugs. They had a man sent off, Dracula I think, and we won comfortably enough 2-0.

We lost 1-0 in London, as usual, this time to Spurs, but beat Ipswich 2-0 ahead of the return leg in Romania. All I remember about that trip was the food. It was absolutely terrible. You didn't take your own food abroad in those days and there were no special cooks or teams of dieticians like they have today.

The main thing I remember about the food on away trips is that they always gave you veal, morning, noon and night. I wasn't that keen and got bloody sick of the sight of it. But you had to eat what they gave you at the hotel. In Romania it was mostly cabbage, sausage and garlic. Believe me, it was poor.

We had to kick off early because the old stadium, which looked like it should have been condemned, didn't have floodlights. It was a wee little shit hole.

And this was supposed to be the European Cup – the most prestigious competition in the world!

But the bottom line was that they had won their league and that's why they were playing us. We didn't know anything about them and that worried me a bit. It was a poor country and we knew they would be running their socks off to try and impress and get a move abroad. I would have rather been up against players who were in the comfort zone – they didn't have to try so much.

I don't know if we were still running off the effects of all that garlic and sausage, but we lost 4-1 at Southampton back in the League with Francis in for O'Hare as the only change. To make matters worse I broke my nose. Mick Channon had arms line a windmill and I ran into his elbow ….. splat.

It wasn't his fault. It was an accident. But they couldn't stop the bleeding and I was out for four games. I had two black eyes into the bargain. I looked like a Giant Panda and had to have a cast on my nose and about a mile of cotton wool stuffed up my hooter. It was a nightmare and ruined my good looks!

Now Nottingham Forest conceding four goals? It just didn't happen. But it did happen again, and at struggling Derby of all places

– after we had lost our long unbeaten home record, 1-0 to another struggling side, Brighton. Robbo, uncharacteristically, missed a penalty.

Little did we know that it was also the last time we would see Tony Woodcock. I don't know the full story but I think Tony had been in to ask for more money. As usual, the gaffer was playing his mind games and turned him down. Unfortunately, Cologne had been sniffing around for sometime and Tony agreed terms with them. The gaffer finally agreed to match them but, by then, Tony had given his word and it was too late. He was off to Germany where he became something of a super-star. Good luck to him, but I was sorry to see him go. It left a wee bit of a hole.

Another link in the chain had gone. And all Forest had to show for it was £650,000 transfer fee, which was the limit in those days.

It had been a bad few days and the gaffer took the lads out to Egypt to get away from it all for a bit, but I didn't go. I stayed behind for treatment, along with John O'Hare. The lads went to see the pyramids and all that, but I've never been one for sightseeing. I'd normally head for the nearest bar. I missed five games, including a friendly at Plymouth, and Dave Needham again replaced me in the side.

I was back for the 1-1 draw with Arsenal, a late Birtles goal salvaging a point. We drew 0-0 at Second Division West Ham in the quarter-finals of the League Cup and lost 1-0 at promoted Palace before beating West Ham 3-0 after extra-time in the replay. John O'Hare had a great game in the mud and rain that night. He broke the deadlock in the 99th minute to finally beat Phil Parkes and then Birtles and O'Neill killed them off. I had a hand in the third, picking out O'Hare who threaded a fine ball through for O'Neill. West Ham played well but David Cross and Stuart Pearson got no change out of me and Larry.

It was our 23rd match in the competition without defeat. But something was wrong. Yes, we were missing Woodcock, but we hadn't really replaced Archie in midfield. There was talk of Martin O'Neill being sent to Coventry in exchange for Mick Ferguson – fortunately that fell through – and we knew Peter had been "spying" on a couple of players. What we didn't expect was that one of them was Stan Bowles. Yes, Stan Bowles! Now Stan had a worse reputation than me and was on the list at QPR for £250,000 with no hint of a taker.

He liked a gamble, to put it mildly, and he also liked a drink. He loved the champagne lifestyle and his best England days seemed to be a long way behind him. Certainly not the type to fit in at Forest, was he? The gaffers had considered Peter Ward and Mick Ferguson but, for whatever reason, gambled on Stan the Man instead.

He made his debut, in place of John O'Hare, in a friendly with Cologne, arranged as part of the Woodcock transfer, and took about 20 seconds to fit in. He made his League debut against Man United, who were level on points with Liverpool at the top. But we were unable to improve on our wretched away form and were 3-0 down at the break.

Stan scored the winner at home to Villa and notched again in a very satisfying 3-0 win at Coventry. Sadly, they were to be the only goals he scored.

Typically, we then lost 1-0 at Everton and beat Leeds 4-1 away in the 3rd round of the FA Cup, Frank Gray scoring with a free-kick after about a minute of his return to Elland Road.

I played in a friendly at Gravesend after that and again the gaffer put out a full strength side, with the exception of Jim Montgomery in for Shilton in goal.

Jim was a good keeper, a hero for Sunderland in their FA Cup epic with Leeds. He seemed an odd choice as an understudy to Shilts, but I think he knew the gaffer from his days at Sunderland. He was a quiet lad and looked a bit like Clarence the cross-eyed lion. But he was still a good keeper and you could rely on him to do a job.

I sat out the next four - the 3-1 win over West Brom, the 2-1 win at Leeds and two games against Liverpool. While I was out Charlie George had arrived on loan from Southampton.

Like Stan, he was an entertainer and a showman and he had bags and bags of skill. Apparently, Cloughie had been after him for years, but was put off by the £500,000 asking price. It's a shame he only played four games for us because he knew how to look after himself and was certainly something special.

I had played against him before but didn't realise how tall he was. To be fair to him, he didn't come for a holiday and played in both legs of the Super Cup against Barcelona. He had an amazing talent. I did not realise just how good he was until I played alongside him. He was so good that he wouldn't have looked out of place in the Brazil team. I can't pay him a higher compliment than that.

We managed to sneak a 1-0 home win over Liverpool in the first leg of the League Cup thanks to a late Robbo penalty. Four days later we played them in the 4th round of the FA Cup and lost 2-0 courtesy of a rare error by Shilts and a penalty.

Fortunately, I was back for the European Super Cup games against Barcelona. We won the home leg 1-0 with an 11th-minute goal from George, on his debut. The muddy pitch didn't make for a good game but this time Larry and me combined to find Charlie. He slung the ball out to Trevor Francis and then got on the end of the return cross to head into the far corner.

I then set up Francis and he should have done better than hit the woodwork. Stan Bowles was also denied by the woodwork; keeper Artola made a good save from me and I also headed over. It should have been more than 1-0 but we were champions of Europe and were confident it would be enough - even though we could be without six players because of the European Championships game between England and Scotland.

There were almost 100,000 fanatical fans crammed in there for the return leg and it was like a cauldron in the Nou Camp. It was unbelievable and I was in awe of the place. It had what you might call the 'Wow Factor'. They even had a chapel for the players. It was a real eye-opener for me.

I had never really bothered about playing in front of big crowds before, but this was something else. It was just amazing and is one of my lasting memories.

I thought we had scored early doors when Garry Birtles had the ball in the net, but Francis was penalised for hands. Barcelona's European Footballer of the Year, Allan Simonsen, also had a goal disallowed for a foul on Shilts.

Barcelona took the lead with a penalty after a foul by Frank Gray on Simonsen. But we didn't panic. Robbo was giving them all kinds of problems and although Golden Bollocks was quiet, Stan the Man fancied it a bit that night, despite getting a kicking from a chap called Olmo.

Stan won us a penalty when Olmo tripped him but Robbo, uncharacteristically, put his kick too close to the advancing keeper, who had clearly moved early.

Shilts made three or four good saves from Simonsen but I managed to grab the equaliser. Larry flicked a Robbo corner on at the near post and I nodded it in. I've scored better, but it was a great feeling when it hit the back of the net. That shut the fanatical crowd up for a bit and we won 2-1 on aggregate.

The chairman, Geoffrey Macpherson, joined us for the celebration team pictures and the gaffer went barmy. "Don't ever let him on a picture again," he fumed.

Four days later we were being held to a 0-0 draw at home by Bristol City. Talk about after the Lord Mayor's show. But it was just another game to us; another job to do. I didn't matter if you were playing in front of 90,000 at the Nou Camp or two men and a dog, your attitude had to be the same. Simple as that.

Francis, Bowles and George were missing for the return leg with Liverpool and the gaffer gambled by bringing in young Gary Mills – mind you he still looks about 18 these days – and pushing Martin O'Neill up front. Well, he always said he was too good for the No7 shirt. Remarkably, it paid off and Martin won us a penalty, which Robbo tucked away. Super sub David Fairclough scored in the last minute, but it was too late and we were on the way back to Wembley for the third year in a row. Can you believe that?

Liverpool had their revenge in the League a few days later. And although we beat Manchester City 4-0 with a Francis hat-trick, our dismal away form continued with a 1-0 defeat at Bolton. Not the kind of result you want with a vital European Cup tie against a Dynamo Berlin side, packed with internationals, on the horizon.

Bryn Gunn came in for Viv, who was suspended. Unfortunately, the Germans produced a classic away performance and snatched a

1-0 win through Riediger after Stan had given the ball away. It could have been worse, but for Peter Shilton. We weren't happy to say the least, and Spurs copped it a few days later when we smashed them 4-0. I think I got two that day, while Francis got the other two. Wolves must have been wetting themselves when they saw that result ahead of the League Cup final.

But John Barnwell, who had been a Forest favourite, had done a good job with Wolves. He had splashed out on Andy Gray, who was a handful for any centre-half and brought in Emlyn Hughes, sadly no longer with us, from Liverpool. We were without Larry Lloyd who was suspended for one match, but had no fears about David Needham coming in again, even though he wasn't a nasty bastard like Larry.

There was a superb gesture from the gaffers about 20 minutes before the kick off when they told Jimmy Gordon to lead the team out. He was taken completely by surprise and didn't even have time to get changed. Some people thought BC was sticking two fingers up to the powers that be, but he wasn't. This one was a 'thank you' to good old Jimmy.

Forest hadn't lost a League Cup game for three seasons yet this was one of those games when we did everything but score past keeper Paul Bradshaw. We were playing with a new type of ball, which didn't help. Then disaster struck. They hit a hopeful long ball forward and instead of heading it clear, Needham tried to chest it back to Shilton.

Unfortunately Shilts had also decided to come for the ball. They collided on the edge of the box and Andy Gray – who had hardly had a kick - nipped in to score the softest of goals you will ever see. Shilts says he shouted for the ball but, if he did, Needham never heard him above the roar of the crowd. I never heard Shilts call – he was never a shouter. Shilts blamed the bad bounce of the new ball, but I blamed him. If a goalkeeper comes off his line he has to get the ball. That's his job. End of story.

We didn't have too much time to mourn the loss of the Cup because we had the 2nd leg of the European Cup at a freezing-cold Berlin to worry about next. I was suspended and didn't make the trip but I heard that they'd just won their last game 10-0, the stadium was a right dump. I'd had a right result there. Fortunately, that night Francis paid back a big slice of that £1m transfer fee. He was inspired – perhaps he had to run about a bit more or freeze to death. Either way he scored two goals and Robbo added a penalty as we won 3-1.

It was still a case of win one at home, lose one away in the League however. And, four days before we were due to face the mighty Ajax in the European Cup, we lost 3-2 at Villa. Now if we couldn't beat Villa how the hell were we going to cope with three-times European Champions Ajax, who had scored 30 goals on the way to the semi-finals?

But we had always wanted to test ourselves against one of the big guns of Europe. Now we had the chance. We needn't have worried because we won 2-0 with a Francis tap-in, when the keeper dropped the ball, and a Robbo penalty, after a defender handled under pressure.

We were still in demand for lucrative friendlies and we flew out for a bit of sun in the Middle East, beating an Emirates side 4-0 and Murrahaq 8-2. Francis got five of the goals. We also had a testimonial at Lincoln for their physio, Bert Loxley, which I managed to avoid through suspension.

It attracted a gate of 6,000 – twice their normal crowd. But the wisdom of playing these friendlies was brought into question again when Trevor Francis injured his hip in the 1-2 defeat. He fell awkwardly and was pulled off straight away. Shilts was also missing – he was playing in a testimonial in Stoke for Denis Smith.

I also missed the 1-0 win over struggling Derby County, which just about condemned the Rams to relegation.

The night before the big return with Ajax, Cloughie took us for a walk as usual. But this time it was round the famous – or is it infamous? – red light district for a bit of team bonding. We had a right laugh outside one sex club while Peter Taylor pretended to get us in on the cheap as a block booking. We went inside one club for a couple of beers and who was sitting there? None other than the Forest chairman!

I met up with my old mate from Birmingham, Jimmy Calderwood, who had been working in Holland for many years. We sat in the corner of the bar having a drink and Cloughie was buying the beers. I introduced him to Jimmy and he bought him a drink. After a while he came over and said to Jimmy: "You've had your drink, now piss off."

Ajax hadn't been beaten at home in Europe for 46 games and because of the demand for tickets the match had been switched to the Olympic Stadium.

We defended superbly that night, hoping to get an away goal. In the end Peter Shilton was finally beaten when Soren Lerby headed in a corner, but we went through 2-1 on aggregate.

The cup runs meant that we had fallen behind in our fixtures but we went on a good run of three wins and two draws. Needham came in for me for the 0-0 draw with Middlesbrough but I was back for the wins over Norwich (2-0) and Palace (4-0) and the 0-0 draw at Arsenal.

Francis had bagged two goals against Palace and was going for his hat-trick when he suddenly fell over. He had ruptured his Achilles tendon – a career-threatening injury in those days. He was out for the season.

I had a run out up front alongside John O'Hare in the 2-1 County Cup final win over Notts County (although I ended up back in central defence in the second half). Some fans question the wisdom on the County Cup, which usually draws small crowds, but they are competitive games and, again, it's better than training.

Don't forget, Notts had a good side in those days with a young Brian Kilcline alongside Brian Stubbs at the back and Masson and McCulloch in midfield. And Robbo still says that the late Pedro Richards was one of the hardest he'd ever played against.

O'Hare scored a good goal after only seven minutes, although some thought he was off-side and Robbo got the second from the penalty spot. Paul Hooks pulled one back near the end when he skipped past Larry and Dave Needham and calmly beat the advancing Jim Montgomery.

I was back in the No6 shirt for the 1-0 home win over Everton and the friendlies with Stade Brestois (1-0) and Leicester (0-0). But the Stade game was the last the fans saw of Stan Bowles, who walked out on the club after being dropped.

But two weeks before the European Cup Final we went down 3-1 at Wolves. I had a bad day at the office - and it could have been more if not for the brilliance of Peter Shilton. Wolves had gone close as early as the fourth minute through Kenny Hibbitt and 60 seconds later I brought down Andy Gray. Hibbitt tucked away the penalty. John Richards got the second and I made another mistake for Geoff Palmer's goal after 83 minutes when Mel Eaves got the better of me and that was me done. I was off and David Needham was brought on.

We flew off to the sun for a break in Cala Millor before the final with Hamburg at Real Madrid's superb Bernabeu stadium. We took things easy, as usual, because we couldn't find any grass to train on. The sun-baked ground was rock hard and Shilts, who was carrying an injury, ended up stopping shots on a traffic island after being kicked off the lawn at the hotel. Shilts, who was never injured, had done his calf muscle and needed a pain-killing injection before he played.

Larry had stayed behind in England to get treatment and Frank Gray was also struggling a bit. Francis was out and we were so short of players that we could only muster four subs for the game, which was our 80th that season, instead of five – Jim Montgomery, Bryn Gunn, David Needham and John O'Hare.

Typically Larry told Cloughie he was fit to play. Typically the gaffer didn't believe a word he said and aimed a few kicks at Larry's bad ankle during a game of five-a-side. The squad was down to the bare bones and here was the manager trying his best to crock our centre-half ahead of what was, potentially, perhaps the most vital game in the club's history. Larry's ankle came up like a balloon and he spent the afternoon with his leg stuck in a bucket of ice.

We were the underdogs this time. Hamburg were a quality side with some big names, plus little Kevin Keegan, the European Football of the Year who wanted to go out on a high note before joining Southampton. Larry did his best to unsettle him in the tunnel. He told Keegan that my job was to try and break him in two and basically kick the shit out of him every time he went near the ball.

Then Larry pointed him in my direction, just as I was taking my teeth out. I always did before I went to work.

It was my job to keep Keegan quiet. We went for a 50-50 ball. Crunch. We both went down but he got up and, to his credit, the little bugger came back for some more. Then I caught him a couple of good ones and told him that I would soon be coming back to give him another helping – or words to that effect. He dropped further and further back after that. Job done.

But we were under a lot of pressure and had to leave Garry Birtles on his own up front. He ran miles and miles that night. He was getting tackled from behind and got no protection from the ref. Gaz was tremendous and even managed to set up the vital goal for Robbo in the 21st minute.

It was backs to the wall again after that with Shilts at his very best. John O'Hare came on for the tiring Gary Mills and to make matters worse Frankie Gray came off injured and the untried Bryn Gunn had to come on for a nervous last few minutes. But we were champions of Europe AGAIN.

I think it is probably the best game I've ever played in.

The two gaffers disappeared down the tunnel leaving us to celebrate with a lap of honour. And, in contrast to the Malmo game, boy did we celebrate.

Back at the hotel we were told to drink what we liked and as much as we liked for as long as we liked. But, under no circumstances were we to go out.

But, after a couple of hours, I was bored. I ordered a taxi and climbed out of a window. Me, Larry, Robbo, Martin and Viv went out on the town.

At about one in the morning I went to see my wife, Louise, who was staying at a different hotel. I ordered some champagne and decided it was time to have a party in her room.

At about 2.30am the door swung open and the chairman, Fred Reacher, poked his head inside. I said: "You haven't seen me, have you Mr Chairman?" "Right," said Fred. I got back to the hotel at about 7am, I couldn't remember where it was. All I knew was that it was somewhere high up in the mountains. One or two of the lads were already down in the bar when I crept in and joined them. Great. I had got away with it. Or so I thought. About 20 years later I was having a drink with the gaffer when he said "You were one of the buggers that sneaked out of the hotel, weren't you?" He'd known all the time. We got an even bigger reception this time when we got back to the East Midlands airport and got another brilliant civic reception in the old market square. The fans were absolutely fantastic. Those memories will stay with me until the day I die.

I'm often asked at dinners what the highlight at Forest was for me. The answer is easy: the whole four years. There wasn't one day when I didn't look forward to going into work and I didn't like training. But it was just great fun. We used to take the piss out of each other; the banter was great. Everything we did was so much fun that the time whizzed by.

Larry gets in on the action against Barcelona in the Super Cup

My equaliser sealed it for Forest. We beat Barcelona 2-1 on aggregate

Me, John McGovern and Stan Bowles take a look at the Super Cup silverware

Chairman Geoffrey Macpherson got in on the act, which upset the Gaffer

Andy Gray, who scored the winner in the League Cup final

Our second European Cup win, but Robbo was not a happy man after being told we couldn't leave the hotel that night

I fight off Viv to get my hands on the cup for the second season in a row

How would today's players cope with a pitch like this?

The beginning of the end
(1980-1982)

I suppose 1980-81 was the season things started to go sour for us –
even though we finished seventh in the league. Larry Lloyd, Martin
O'Neill and John O'Hare all departed…. and we finished without a
major trophy for once.

We had a busier pre-season than usual, with games in North
America against Vancouver Whitecaps, Tampa Bay Rowdies, a
Colombia X1 and Toronto Blizzard. We also played in Paddy
Mulligan's Testimonial, plus outings against Alkmaar AZ67, Bayern
Munich and Grasshopper Zurich.

America was good trip. The scenery, like Niagara Falls, was
awesome (although I spent most of the time playing cards on the
coach) and the pitches were very good.

But it was an exhausting trip. I thought it was a long way to go
for a game of football, but it did give Ian Wallace the perfect chance
to bed in. I had been instrumental in bringing him to the club and I
just hoped he would repay his £1,250,000 transfer fee with a few
goals.

I had no worries about him because he shielded the ball well and
was busy in the six-yard box. He loved to score goals and didn't care
if they went in off his elbow or his arse, as long as they went in.

Wallace played in the first game, a 1-1 draw with Vancouver who
were managed by Tony Waiters and had players of the calibre of Ray
Hankin (Leeds), Dutchman Rudi Krol, Derby pair Kevin Hector and
Trevor Whymark and Alan Taylor (West Ham). A crowd of 28,710
watched the game – a record for an exhibition match.

John McGovern scored after 15 minutes, but then made way for
Raimondo Ponte, who had been brought in from Grasshoppers for
£230,000. I thought it was a lot of money for a player of his calibre
and I think he only lasted about 17 games before he was shipped off
to France.

It was blowing a gale and lashing down with rain before the Tampa game with trees almost being bent double. I thought there was no chance of playing, but the pitch was perfect. The only trouble was that the match was sponsored by a firm that made organs and they played loud, annoying, organ music for the entire game. Still, some of the scantily-clad cheer leaders weren't too bad. It was interesting to say the least.

We drew 0-0 with Tampa, who were managed by Gordon Jago. But then lost 5-0, would you believe, to the Colombian national team, in Bogotá. We were 4-0 down at the break I think and there were a few ructions in the dressing room along the lines of "What the hell are we doing here?" We were jet-lagged and coach-lagged and playing 8,000ft above sea level. I gave away a penalty and to make matters worse Frank Gray was sent off. We missed Robbo, who had flown home following the death of his father, and Francis and Wallace, who were both injured.

We finally managed a win, beating Toronto Blizzard, before flying home for Paddy Mulligan's testimonial in Ireland. I didn't even know who it was for at first. But the crowd kept getting bigger and bigger before kick-off and we ended playing an all-Ireland team in front of 22,000. Some friendly! But we won 3-2 with goals from Ian Wallace (2) and Garry Birtles.

A 3-0 defeat against Bayern Munich and a 0-0 draw with Grasshopper Zurich meant we had played eight games in four weeks.

Anyway, we started the season in familiar fashion by losing in London, 2-0 in front of a crowd of over 43,000 at Spurs, but beat Birmingham 2-1 in the opening home game.

A 0-0 draw at Everton was followed by a 4-1 aggregate League Cup win over Peterborough and a 5-0 thrashing of Stoke. So far, so good. We had gone seven games without defeat going into the first leg of the European Cup at Bulgarian champions CSKA Sofia.

But we lost 1-0 to a goal from Yonchev, after Robbo saw a shot come back off the inside of a post. I limped off at half-time with a thigh injury which kept me out for the next four games. We ended up going out 2-0 on aggregate. Forest, champions for the past two years, had fallen at the first hurdle. The glory days were over.

In between we beat Leicester City 5-0 and Bury 7-0 in the League Cup. Things continued to go well in the League despite a 2-1 home defeat by Man United. After the game Garry Birtles, who had developed into one of the best centre-forwards in the country, signed for United for £1,250,000.

We drew 2-2 at Sunderland and pipped Brighton 1-0 at home before a friendly with Tampa, which we won 7-1. I played up front in that one and bagged a goal, while young Mills got a hat-trick. We beat West Brom 2-1 and then Peter Ward, who cost £400,000, made his debut in place of Birtles in the 2-1 home win over Leeds.

Peter Taylor had been after Ward, who started out in Sunday League football in Derby, for some time. I don't think Brian Clough fancied him that much, but Peter must have talked him into it. He played 12 games, including a friendly at Grantham, when Francis finally came back. I thought Ward was a little light-weight but he was confident enough. He had a few tricks and certainly had an eye for goal when he was in the penalty box.

But he wasn't as good as Birtles, or Withe for that matter, and there were more disappointments on the horizon as we crashed 4-1 at Watford in the 4th round of the League Cup. Steve Sutton was deputising for Shilton but, other than that, we pretty much had a full-strength side. I gave away a penalty, which gave them a lift and it was an uphill battle after that.

We bounced back to beat Southampton 2-1 at home through Ward and Robbo, with Shilts back between the sticks, and drew 0-0 at Liverpool before losing three in a row, against Birmingham (0-2), Spurs (0-3) and Ipswich (1-2). Hardly the ideal tonic before the Super Cup game with European Cup Winners Cup winners Valencia, but we won 2-1 with two from Ian Bowyer in front of a crowd of only 12,463. Perhaps the fans thought it was just a glorified friendly. But Valencia were anything but friendly. The referee was weak and booked five players. We went 1-0 down after 46 minutes but Bowyer grabbed the equaliser after 57 minutes from a Ward cross. In the final minute Lloyd header down a Mills' corner and Bomber scored at the far post.

There was no love lost in the return at the Luis Casanova Stadium either. Ian Bowyer, Robbo, Frank Gray and Gary Mills were all missing. But it was good to see Trevor Francis back after his Achilles tendon injury – no, really, it was – and he came in for some tough treatment. I was also lucky to get away with a couple of bad tackles and foul on Saura in the box, which sparked a volley of fire-crackers from the volatile crowd.

Raimondo Ponte wasted a good chance when he shot straight at the keeper and Shilts made a cracking save from Argentinean World Cup star Mario Kempes. But he was beaten when a shot came back off the bar and Morena tapped the rebound into the net.

Despite the best efforts of Francis we lost 1-0 and Valencia took the trophy on the away goals rule.

So, in the space of a couple of months were had lost our grip on the European Cup and now the Super Cup.

Back in the League things were going well, however. We beat Sunderland (3-1) with goals from Ponte, Francis and Walsh and Wolves (4-1) away and drew 2-2 at home to Villa. We beat Bolton 1-0 in the FA Cup after being held 3-3 at home. Larry was injured after that and only played one more game. We drew 3-3 with Bolton in the FA Cup but won the replay 1-0.

We then had a friendly with Paris St Germain, which we lost 2-0. I was sub that night, but I was desperate to play when I saw the magnificent stadium. We pipped Manchester United 1-0 in the FA Cup and Everton 1-0 at home in the League before entertaining Red Star Belgrade, who were on a five-match tour of Britain, in a friendly. We lost 3-1 – another reminder, as if we needed it, that we were no longer the Kings of Europe. They were sharper and quicker than us and it was perhaps just as well that there were only 10,000 there to witness it.

We drew 1-1 at Manchester City before we took on a South American team Nacional, in the World Club championship in Tokyo.

We stopped off at Anchorage on the way because the flight was so long. Tokyo was manic. Watching the traffic flash by was like looking at ants in a garden. And I think our bus driver had been trained by Evil Knievel.

We were all shattered from the trip and wanted to go to bed at 10 o'clock but Cloughie wouldn't let us. "We are going to keep to British time," he said. "It's six o'clock back home." We had to go for a drink but, for once, we would rather have got some kip. But we were ok for the game.

We did some light training the following day and played Nacional, who had been resting up since their season ended in October, on the Wednesday on a dry, bumpy pitch in front of a crowd of 62,000 at the plush Olympic Stadium.

Nacional were nothing special and we absolutely pummelled them.

John McGovern was out through injury and Stuart Gray, who took his place, headed against the post. Robbo headed wide and Ian Wallace shot wide. We dominated the game but failed to take our chances and lost 1-0 to a goal only ten minutes into the first-half.

Larry Lloyd, back in the side after missing six games with a hamstring strain had penalty appeals turned down when a defender appeared to handle his header. We played well but couldn't beat their packed defence. It was just one of those days.

We carved out the best chances and also hit the woodwork twice but we should have won.

Trevor Francis played well in the heat, yet Cloughie said he thought I was the Man of the Match. However, the Japanese journalists gave it to the goal scorer, star Uruguayan striker Valdemar Victorino. He only had a couple of kicks all night and won a brand new car. But it wasn't a bad effort, I'll give him that. Moreira got in a cross that eluded Larry Lloyd and Victorino got around me to slide a shot past Shilts from seven or eight yards. Shilts made a good save to deny Victorino a second, but they held on to win despite the efforts of Francis, Wallace and sub Peter Ward, who came on for Ponte.

Sadly, it was to be Larry's last game. He left to become player-manager of Wigan. It was a wrench to see him go because we'd been a good double act for the past three years.

I shared the centre-half duties with Needham and Einar Jan Aas after that. Big Einar was a good lad. A Norwegian international, he had played in midfield against Scotland. He spoke better English then me, but I don't think his style of play was suited to English football.

He was far too nice for a start. If he did a bad tackle he would go over and apologise. You had to be a wee bit nasty in those days and Larry would have told them to piss off. Larry did not take any shit from anybody. That's why he fell out so much with the gaffer, I suppose. Larry wanted to show that he was big and brave enough to stand up to BC.

It's a toss up who had the biggest head…but there was only ever going to be one winner and it wasn't Larry.

We went on a good little run after that. Three days later we beat Bristol City 2-1 in the 5th round of the FA Cup with goals from Wallace and Robbo. We were jet-lagged after arriving back in London in the early hours of Friday morning and were 1-0 down with 15 minutes to go.

We then chalked up League wins over Stoke (2-1), Arsenal (3-1) through O'Neill (2) and me, then Middlesbrough (1-0), with another goal from yours truly. I'd been having a few games in the No5 shirt and I think Peter Taylor fancied me as a centre-half. I'm not saying I couldn't do it, but I wasn't six feet nine was I?

Stuart Gray, Aas, Mills, Colin Walsh and Gunn were getting more games now. They showed promise but they were nowhere as good as the men they were replacing.

The secret to Forest's success over the last few years was that we had been basically playing the same side week in week out.

Ipswich were next up in the Cup but we could only draw 3-3 at home and lost the replay 1-0 after Ian Wallace had a second-minute goal disallowed. We had been the better side, even with teenagers Colin Walsh and Gary Mills in midfield. But fussy Clive Thomas booked Bryn Gunn, Stuart Gray and John Robertson, along with three from Ipswich. Arnold Muhren got the killer goal in the 68th minute.

It meant that, for the first time since 1978, we would not be at Wembley.

I managed to get on the score sheet again in the next game with Brighton at home and we drew 1-1 at Man United, in front of 38,000 thanks to another goal from my mate Wallace. I scored a bizarre own goal that night. I stretched out a leg to concede a corner but the wind caught the ball and it swerved past Shilts and dropped under the bar.

I shouldn't have been playing really. I had been coughing and spluttering all week and couldn't breathe properly. I hadn't trained but I was captain at the time, in place of the injured John McGovern, and didn't want to miss the match.

We lost 2-1 to West Brom who had a cracking squad (Godden, Trewick, Statham, Moses, Wile, Robertson, Robson, Deehan, Bennett, Barnes, Batson, Mills) and beat Norwich for once, 2-1 with two more from Francis.

April started with a 2-0 defeat at Southampton where I collected my fifth booking of the season. I was one of seven booked.

With nothing left to play for we finished seventh in the First Division after a 1-1 draw at Coventry.

I played up front instead of Trevor Francis, who was rested, in the County Cup against Mansfield. We scraped a 2-1 win with an 85th-minute goal from Stuart Gray and I set up the first goal for Peter Ward who side-footed the ball past Steve Sutton. Russ Allen, who I had played against as a kid, scored the Mansfield goal after a slip by David Needham.

I kept my place for the friendly against Notts County but reclaimed the No6 shirt for the friendly with Real Madrid.

But I was not happy about the way the team was being broken up. Garry Birtles had long since gone to Manchester United, Martin O'Neill left for Norwich and Ian Bowyer went to Sunderland, both for £250,000 fees, Frank Gray (£300,000) left for Leeds ahead of me, John O'Hare retired and Larry, of course, had gone into management.

Pre-season 1981-1982 was a mixed bag. We played Linfield in front of a crowd of 5,472 and won 5-1 with a hat-trick from Peter Ward, a Robbo penalty and one from Ian Wallace. We beat Spanish First Division side Osasuna Pamplona 2-1 and drew 1-1 with Real Zaragosa in front of 36,000 thanks to a goal from Mark Proctor, who had finally arrived from Middlesbrough for a big fee. Then there were over 50,000 watching the 0-0 draw with Naples. Proctor wasn't a bad player but he never really settled.

I played at the back with Needham, Gunn and big Einar Aas, who had come in from Bayern Munich. Jurgen Rober also got a few games in We kicked off with a 2-1 home win over Southampton with two from Francis. But it was one of only ten home wins as we finished 12th – our lowest position since the return to Division One.

One problem was Justin Fashanu, who had cost the gaffer a bob or two. He was a nightmare and struggled to control a pass. I don't like to speak ill of the dead, but the bottom line was that he just wasn't good enough and Clough & Taylor had, for once, got it wrong.

We drew 0-0 at Manchester United in front of another 50,000-plus crowd. Trevor controversially signed for their neighbours, Manchester City, for £1,2000,000 before there was an unhappy return to Birmingham for me. Ian Wallace got a hat-trick, but we somehow contrived to lose the match 4-3.

We had a 0-0 home draw with West Brom and beat Stoke 2-1 away with goals from Mills and Wallace. The good run continued with a 2-0 home win over Sunderland and I even managed to bag a goal in the 2-1 win over Brighton.

But we lost 3-0 at Spurs, as usual, and I played my final League game on October 6, a 3-2 League Cup win over Birmingham, before joining Leeds.

After me, John McGovern went to Bolton on a free, Shilts was transferred to Southampton for £325,000 and Gary Mills joined Derby. That just left Viv and Robbo from the glory boys. It was the end of an era….

My goal in the 7-1 friendly win over Tampa Bay Rowdies

Super Cup final against Valencia

Dejection in the Super Cup final. We lost on the away goal rule

Sharing a joke with Cloughie during a stop-over in Anchorage on the way to Japan

Clough & Taylor

Brian Clough and Peter Taylor were unique. Absolutely special. They belonged together like gin and tonic. A great double act, they achieved something that will never be beaten.

It should be the Clough & Taylor stands at Derby and Forest, because, the truth is, they did it together.

It's a fact that the boss was never quite the same without Peter by his side – yet some hardly acknowledge the massive part he played. I certainly owe him a lot.

Peter spotted the players; Brian moulded them into a team. Clough & Taylor taught you good habits and made sure you kept your feet on the ground. They kept it simple and let you get on with your game. I grew up very quickly at Forest. I soon learned the Do's and Don'ts in life and what was acceptable and what wasn't.

It's no coincidence that so many who played under the pair went into management. Frank Clark, Roy McFarland, Dave Mackay, Martin O'Neill, Colin Todd, Larry Lloyd, John McGovern, even Trevor Francis and Peter Shilton, the list is endless.

To be fair, we never saw that much of the pair during the week, they rarely came to training. And there was no point going knocking on the office door, because there would be no-one in.

Sometimes Cloughie would take the dog for a walk and suddenly appear from behind a tree and shout: "Hey you, pass the bloody thing." That was BC.

Their secret was that they never asked a player to try and do what he couldn't do. Let's be honest, John Robertson couldn't tackle fish and chips. But what he could do was receive the ball when we were under pressure; hold it up for two or three seconds and give us some breathing space; time to regroup. Asa Hartford, during his brief spell at the City Ground, once asked Cloughie why he kept telling him to give the ball to Robbo all the time. "Because he's a better player than you and he knows what to do with it," came the reply.

True, the boss could be cruel sometimes - few escaped his

sarcasm. He was a one-off and you never really knew what he would do next, kiss a copper, slap a fan, give an old lady a lift, he did all these types of things.

He certainly didn't suffer fools gladly and he didn't have much time for injured players. When two of the lads, John McGovern and Archie Gemmill, came in limping after a game against West Brom he said: "If you are looking for sympathy look it up in a dictionary, it's right next to shit."

If you were injured, BC didn't even want you in the dressing room before a match. He'd say: "What are you doing here? Fuck off, you are no good to me."

Once, when Larry Lloyd was injured he threw him out of the office and told him not to come back until he was off his crutches. He used to drag players off the treatment table and tell them to go for a walk down the Trent, even if it was pouring with rain. He said the fresh air and exercise would do you more good than lying under a heat lamp. But he was the best manager I ever worked with. He was a dream.

I never had a dad, but Brian Clough was very much a father figure to me. Not only did he make me a better player, I also think he made me a better man.

I cannot fault the man. Every minute spent with him was unforgettable. Respect, Admiration. Yes, he commanded all that.

He's been called arrogant, a conceited tyrant, a bully. People are entitled to their opinion, but they didn't know the real Clough. He certainly had a soft side and was devoted to his wife and family.

Before I came to the club, Cloughie was quoted as saying: "I don't want troublemakers. I don't want shithouses and I don't want an ugly sod like Kenny Burns littering up my football club."

But I had a great rapport with the gaffer, I really did. He was a man's man and liked players with a bit of fire in their belly. In Austria, once, Peter Withe had his nose broken and things were getting a bit tasty. It was a tight little ground and I put one of their players straight through a fence. He came out looking like a chip.

I was expecting to hear "Kenneth" and a rollicking from the boss when things calmed down. Instead, he gave me the thumbs up.

Typical! Yes, he had a harsh tongue. But he was joking most of the time - I think! The day he signed me he said: "I might want to sell you again." And I replied "Yes, if you get fed up with winning trophies." I'll never forget that.

I was supposed to have a bad boy tag but he wasn't bothered – just as long as I did the business on the pitch. Before one match he shouted: "Kenneth. The No10, no pads." Which was his way of saying give him a kick on the shins.

He could make you laugh and he could also have you in tears. Yes, I miss him and Peter. I think of them a lot.

I couldn't believe it when I found out Peter Taylor had died suddenly. I couldn't bring myself to go to the funeral. I did my grieving in private.

I'm not ashamed to admit that I've shed tears for both of them.

I went to Cloughies' memorial service at Pride Park and that was tough. I was in pieces.

But I just couldn't to go to the funeral. I just couldn't.

It was a shame they fell out. Relations had become strained over some of the expensive signings, which had flopped. Taylor was also unhappy that Cloughie had turned down the chance to go back to Derby without telling him. And he wasn't best pleased when he found out Cloughie had copped for a big pay rise while he got nothing.

Cloughie, for his part, fell out with Peter when he wrote a book without telling him.

But the final straw came when Peter signed Robbo on Cup Final day when BC was away on a charity walk with Alan Hill. As far as I know they never did make up. Cloughie even banned Robbo from the City Ground for bit.

I prefer to picture Cloughie in his prime at Forest. But I do think he stayed at the City Ground a year too long and it was very sad to see him at the end. I was at the ground the day after they got relegated and you could almost taste the sadness in the air.

I blame David Platt for a lot of the club's troubles in recent years. The chairman brought him in from Italy and he let him squander a fortune. He brought three Italians along with him – the old boy's act.

He bought a full-back that couldn't tackle; a winger that couldn't cross the road and another who was born injured. He was older than me. They cost millions and I feel that the club went downhill rapidly under him.

Because of Clough & Taylor my time at Forest simply flew by. We just loved playing football. One season I think we clocked up 75 official games, what with testimonial matches and the like. But I never felt tired. We didn't want the season to end.

BC didn't believe in too much training. He wanted to keep us fresh. He would tell us to take the missus out for a meal instead. Go away for the day; have a drink, have sex, relax, have a rest. Whatever you do, don't do any training. Don't come in until Thursday. He'd have us visiting hospitals, going for walks, anything to take our minds off the next game.

Before a big game he would have us drinking champagne and beer. "It's good for you. You will sleep better with a beer in you," he would say.

You never knew what the next the day would bring at Forest. Once we turned up for training and Jimmy Gordon told us not to bother getting changed. We got on a bus and ended at Scarborough of all places. We had a 20 minute walk along the front to the hotel where 15 steaks and a couple of beers were waiting for us. We had another 20-minute walk and got home about 7 o'clock that night. I thought it had been a bit of a waste of time until I found out the real reason for the trip from Albert the bus driver. Peter had wanted to take some carpets and paint to a flat in Scarborough.

Once, while we were training at Bisham Abbey and Ron Fenton told us to do six shuttles. They weren't the love of my life either, but after two Cloughie said "That's enough. Go and play golf or tennis." That night we asked John McGovern if it was all right for us to have a drink. Just then the gaffer came in and asked us for two quid each. "What's this for?" we asked. "It's for the kitty," he said. "I'll have a large Scotch."

It was hard being a pro footballer at Forest in those days!

Sometimes training consisted of a walk down the river bank, which was full of nettles. Cloughie didn't let you wear tracksuit bottoms, hats or gloves. He reasoned that you couldn't play in them so why train in them. Before we got to the nettle patches we rolled our socks right up and tucked our shirts in.

The idea was to get behind Larry Lloyd and let him plough a path through the jungle. On another occasion he had the players punching a tree – even keeper Peter Shilton - on the eve of a big European Cup game.

Most of the time, training just involved a game of five-a-side, which often got a bit tasty, with tackles flying in. I whacked Trevor Francis at every opportunity. There was no vendetta against him. But I got the feeling that he thought he was better than the rest of us. Perhaps it was the burden of that £1m transfer fee.

Cloughie liked to join in now and again. He still thought he could play. I think the last time he joined in was before the European Cup final with Hamburg. We were up in the mountains and it was hailing. I accidentally kicked the ball into his stomach and he doubled up. I can't remember him playing again after that.

He preferred playing tennis with John Lawson, who was the Forest reporter at the local paper, the Nottingham Evening Post at the time, and squash with John McGovern. Cloughie used to cheat like mad at squash and started playing with Garry Birtles when JMcG started to get too good.

After we played in Tokyo, the boss came in with a box full of cash. Big Larry kept an eye on the door while we divided it up. There was £500 for each of us. No doubt Peter and Brian took a few quid for themselves.

Cloughie had the knack of building players up and he could also knock them down. One day we were playing five-a-side at Lady Bay when the gaffer suddenly appeared. He sat everyone down and asked Martin O'Neill what was up with him. "You've been tripping over your face for the last three weeks," said Clough. "We'll sit here all day until you tell us." Martin, who'd been dropped to make way for Trevor Francis, wanted to know why he was in the Reserves and Cloughie replied "Because you are too good for the third team" and then turned and walked away.

Another Clough classic came the night before the League Cup

final with Southampton. The lads were sat drinking beer, wine and champagne. Archie Gemmill had gone to bed to get an early night but the boss phoned him and made him come down for a drink of champagne. Along came six more bottles of bubbly. After that Archie said he still wanted to go to bed, so Cloughie ordered another six. "Very nice boss", said a mellowing Archie. "I could do with some more of that."

"Get to bed you little bastard," barked Cloughie. "Don't you know it's one o'clock and we've got a big game tomorrow."

Some of the lads didn't make breakfast and it looked to have backfired when we went 1-0 down. Cloughie threatened to pull Archie off at half-time, but we won in the end. That was the magic of Brian Clough.

Under him we were afraid of no-one. If anyone got in our way, we just pushed them aside. We were like a Rolls Royce of a team. I think even Brian and Peter were surprised by what we achieved.

I would have loved to have been a fly on the wall in the office when they talked about the trophies we had won.

After all, as Ipswich's Mick Mills said, we were just a load of old has-beens, weren't we?

But Clough & Taylor turned us into a well-oiled machine. From the tea lady to the kit man, they all had their part to play.

Contrary to what you might think, Cloughie didn't have any favourites. People thought John McGovern was the gaffer's pet, but he wasn't. If he ran to take a throw-in he got a right bollocking." I don't pay you to take throw-ins, give it to someone who can play with it," said Clough.

Ten minutes before a match BC would come into the dressing room and sit beside me and shout to Robbo who was having a crafty fag in the toilet. "You smoking in there Robbo?" "Not me boss, I don't smoke."

He never talked about the match. He would sit there with a cigar and blow smoke all over Larry Lloyd. "I do that to annoy the big bastard," he would say.

Maybe Martin and Larry didn't like Clough, but they had the utmost respect for him. Players have been offered thousands over the years to tell stories about him, but they do not want to disrespect his memory.

Cloughie once told Peter Shilton to accompany him to the weekly Press conference and made him serve the drinks to the assembled reporters. Needless to say, it didn't go down to well with Shilts. Maybe it was the gaffer's way of taking him down a peg or two.

And he once fined me £50 for making a bad pass against Manchester City. Shilts had come off his line, which was a first for him, so I tried to play the ball across the 18-yard box to Frank Clark. I didn't quite get enough height on the pass and Dennis Tueart got a touch but, fortunately, it went out for a goal-kick. I put my hand up straight away to say "Sorry" to the lads but it didn't save me from the wrath of Clough. We won the game 3-0 or something. Afterwards Cloughie came up to me and handed me the dreaded envelope with the red tree. Fined £50, thank you very much. In the next game John McGovern rolled the ball to me but I passed it straight to Larry. I said "You kick it, I can't afford another £50 fine."

Even Trevor Francis had to make the tea for the lads – he must have been the most expensive tea boy in the history of the game - and if Robbo did something out of order he got it in the neck.

We were a team. That's what made us great. We expected to go out and win every game – even at places like Anfield. And we went 42 League games without defeat, so we must have been doing something right.

And there was no fear at the City Ground. You cannot play if you are afraid. Maybe the youngsters like Gary Mills, Bryn Gunn and Chris Woods were scared of him. But most of the time we just had a laugh.

The pair were tremendous together. Peter Taylor was a very funny man, the master of the one liner. He was also very mean with money. He was always getting things for free, like televisions and furniture. He loved money. If he owed you a tenner he would pay you £9.50 back, just so he could make something out of the deal.

When we went on away trips we were allowed £8 a day spending money. On one occasion we had been abroad for three days, that's £24 we were due. But we hadn't had a penny. So Larry Lloyd went

to see the secretary, Ken Smales. He'd given Peter all the money –
but he'd obviously just forgotten to pass it on to us!!!

There was plenty of talk in the Press about bungs to play in
friendlies and testimonials – we certainly played in our fair share of
those - and transfer fees. Whatever, the gaffer certainly didn't like
parting with money and most of the players who went in asking for a
rise came out with a flea in their ear.

I went in twice asking for a rise and did ok, or so I thought. The
first time we had won the League Cup and the Championship. I had
been voted Player of the Year and thought I deserved a reward.
Knowing that BC would knock me back, I decided to ask for £350 a
week. He just said "Ok." I walked out of the door punching the air,
until I realised I could have asked for more. Shit.

The following year we won the league and the European Cup so I
thought I would try my luck again. I planned to ask for £850 and
settle for £750. He just said "Ok" again. No argument, nothing. I
walked out elated again, until I realised he'd just done me again.

We used to sort out our bonuses with Cloughie before the start of
the season. We did ok but we had heard that the London clubs were
on £100 a point and £500 for being in the top six, which was much
more than us. So the players' committee, me, Larry Lloyd and John
McGovern, asked to see the gaffer. We knew he wouldn't be giving
money away so we were prepared for a battle. He asked us what we
wanted and we said £75 a point, £200 top six, £250 top three and
£300 if we were top of the league.

"Is that it? Now I'll tell you what you are getting, £25 a point,
£100 top six, £150 top three and £200 top. I'm not rewarding you for
failure. But if you get 53 points I will pay you £1,000 a point. Now
piss off." We finished that season with three wins and a draw and
picked up £7,000 extra. We hardly ever spoke about money, but I
knew what every player earned. I had a mole in the office.

Nothing scared BC – apart from flying. He always liked to sit and
the front and always had a few drinks to calm him down. He also
liked a joke. Once Stan Bowles bought a little rucksack from a shop
with Old Big Head on the back. The gaffer put it on and walked
round the airport with it on his back. Once he caught Viv dusting

himself down with talc after a game. "It doesn't matter how much you put on you'll still be black in the morning," said Clough. It wasn't racist, it was just the type of comment he came out with from time to time.

Early in my time at Forest we were out in Spain having a drink and relaxing in the sun. Sammy Chapman and Ian Bowyer probably did a little too much relaxing and Cloughie found them swimming down a gutter, pissed. A few weeks later he said he wanted volunteers to present awards at a local swimming club – and nominated Sammy and Bomber.

It was sad to see the gaffer in later years. Was he an alcoholic? I honestly couldn't tell you. He'd always liked a drink but I didn't see it as a problem. I like a pint or two. Does that make me an alcoholic? The gaffer liked two or three drinks. Did that make him an alcoholic?

He had an illness and that's a fact. But there was nothing wrong with his brain. I remember going over to a dinner do at Leicester with him. He spoke for an hour and a half and was absolutely brilliant.

He wasn't a drunk. He once got in my car with a bottle of Vodka. He had a little drink near Nottingham and another one on the way to his home.

I heard tales that he used to sneak out of his house near Derby in his pyjamas, wearing that old blue coat, and go for a drink. He didn't have any money on him, but he remembered who had stood him a round the next time he went in.

I think the gaffer's first love was always Derby – I know Peter never wanted to leave the Baseball Ground. But he never spoke about it. They built a great Derby team from nothing. People like Nish, Todd, McFarland, O'Hare and Hector are legends.

There is no one there now fit to lace their boots.

I think it is criminal that the gaffer didn't get the England job in my first season with the club. He certainly thought he'd got it after his interview but the powers that be bottled it. They didn't think they'd be able to handle the gaffer and appointed Ron Greenwood instead. Nice man I suppose, but he wasn't a patch on Cloughie, who, for me, was the best manager in the world. EVER.

The dynamic duo - such a shame they fell out

On the training ground with Del Boy and squash racket

A tearful farewell - Cloughie's last game

At home in retirement

The old boys back together again. Larry's diet is obviously not working

The pride of Europe

We had a lot of fun at Forest. Perhaps it was all the bonding we did on away trips. Mostly, we all got on well and had a right laugh – especially the day we made a record – We've Got The Whole World in our Hands. It's my claim to fame that I've been on Top of the Pops.

We made the record with a local group, Paper Lace. The fans seemed to like it because it got to No.14 in the charts.

A few of us used to meet up after 'training' at McKay's cafe. By the time we had finished there were about a dozen of us having a coffee and a bacon sandwich. It was great for team spirit.

Some of the lads like Tony Woodcock and Viv liked going into the wine bars in Hockley. Larry and Robbo used to pal about, but I didn't like going into Nottingham much. I was a beer man and preferred a quiet country pub to the city lights.

Most of the lads like a flutter and a game of cards and I was the club bookie. On away trips we played three-card brag. Peter Shilton was absolutely useless at it. You could always tell if he had a good hand. He was crap at it. He had some big wins on the horses but lost so much at the bookies that they used to send him Christmas hampers.

We didn't go mad, two quid a time. Ian Bowyer once won £400 on the way down to Norwich – but he probably lost £410 on the way back. It was just a bit of fun.

Once, in Athens, I was playing cards with Ian Bowyer, Chris Woods and Shilts. There was a big pot and Woods was winning when the lights suddenly went out. When they came back Chris found that the money had disappeared.

Stan Bowles was the worst gambler ever. He had a touch of class on the field when he decided to play and he was a great entertainer on the pitch. But the man shouldn't gamble. He wasn't at the City Ground that long but he ended up owing me about £1,500. One day he said he had a hot tip for the Derby from the mysterious 'Major' and asked me to put a bet on for him with my father-in-law, who used to be a bookie. He put £500 quid on the nose on the horse - I think it's still running.

One day we heard that he was on the move and I though I'd better get my money off him but he said it was just paper talk and that he wasn't going anywhere. Of course he was.

Stan said he would leave the money in an envelope at the ground. It is the first time I have ever run back from training but he had been and gone and there was no sign of any envelope. I had a quick shower and headed for a wine bar in town where I thought he might be. Sure enough he was there celebrating with his missus and I grabbed him by the scruff of the neck and marched him upstairs. I parked the car on yellow lines outside the nearest bank and dragged him in. They weren't keen on cashing his cheque but I managed to sweet talk them; took my money and dropped him off at the wine bar. I thanked him for the cash and reminded him that he owed Martin O'Neill about £2,000. I never saw him again. He was off like a shot, leaving his lady sitting downstairs.

Peter Taylor also liked a bet and I used to put them on for him with my father-in-law.

Peter Shilton: Shilts was a good shot stopper and a great trainer. He might have won a record number of England caps and been regarded as one of the best keepers in the world, but he didn't come for crosses and he didn't really command his box as much as he should have. When a keeper comes off his line he has to get the ball. Simple as that. We used to give him a wee bit of stick about that. He wasn't the greatest of kickers either but, for me, he was better than Ray Clemence.

Shilts would train all day if you let him. He spent hours just diving around saving shots with the younger keepers. Crazy.

We used to have a kitty when we went out for a drink. But Shilts didn't bother, he would order champagne for himself. What a tart. But he was a key member of our card school. We wouldn't play without him – he made our wages up! He couldn't bluff at three card brag to save his life. You could tell from his expression what he was holding.

We used to play a few pranks on him, like the day we put weights in his training bag. He took some stick from the lads, especially after being breathalysed by the police after crashing his Jaguar down at Nottingham Racecourse one night. But he saved us at least six to seven points a year. 10/10

Frank Clark: Got to be one of the best free transfer signings ever. Frank came in when Colin Barrett was injured. Old Frank couldn't kick his Gran and hardly ever made it past the halfway line, but what an inspired signing he turned out to be. He was probably looking forward to his pipe and slippers and a coaching job and ended up with a European Cup-winners medal. He knew his limitations and kept it simple. He wasn't the bravest, but not much got past him. He just won the ball and got it to Robbo as soon as he could. He was a crap singer but he was good on the guitar. I was surprised when the took the managers' job, but he made a good fist of it and signing Stan Collymore was a master-stroke. 8/10

Colin Barrett: I played against Colin when I was a lad at Birmingham and he was at Manchester City and he called me an animal afterwards. Another player who never let you down. He had the same injury as Cloughie and, although he battled back to play again, I don't think he was ever the same. What he did for the club should never be forgotten because his goal against Liverpool won us the European Cup. I don't think he got a medal. After the game with Malmo the boss told us to put our medals on the table but he never got mine. I kept it in my pocket. 8/10

Frank Gray: I've known Frank since I was a nipper. A good looking lad and a great player and what a sweet left foot. Superb at dead-ball situations, but rarely got into the 18-yard box. His best days were probably at Leeds. 7/10

Viv Anderson: Spider was one of my favourites. He's the only black player I know who can't dance. A great lad. He had a big, gangly stride, but the boy could play. He ate up the ground and he scored his fair share of the goals. He had a superstition that he didn't want an early touch in a game, so I used to give it to him on purpose, just to annoy him. He was the best full-back in the country at the time and very little got past him - he had legs like Inspector Gadget. Viv and Tony Woodcock were as thick as thieves. They shared a room and we used to fight like mad. Most of the time they won. We used to trash the room. Whose the daddy now lads? 9/10

David Needham: A big, honest lad, he came in when Larry Lloyd broke his toe. He looked like one of the Bee Gees. BC wanted an animal but he turned out to be Mr Nice Guy. But he never let us down and scored some good goals. When Larry was fit again Cloughie said: "If my daughter Elizabeth ever comes home with a young man I'd like to think it is was someone like you. But tomorrow I need a big ugly bastard and that's why Larry is in the team." Turned out to be an astute, and wealthy, businessman. 7/10

Larry Lloyd: My old partner in crime. Like me, he had a lot of pride in keeping a clean sheet. He was an old fashioned stopper who'd had a good career at Liverpool. But I think Nottingham Forest and Cloughie got the best out of Larry. He could be a bit funny at times and I think he had a bit of a chip on his shoulder. Always at loggerheads with the gaffer, but we got on all right – most of the time. We looked after each other's backs and I picked up a lot from him. The bottom line is that he was an honest player. Cloughie said Larry and me were the two ugliest men in football. He wasn't wrong very often, but he was wrong about that. Not surprisingly, Larry went into the pub business when he retired after a spell in management. Lives in Spain now, but we still keep in touch. 9/10

Archie Gemmill: Archie really made his name at the Baseball Ground where he simply skated over the muddy surface. He had a lot of energy, I'll give him that, but I think he was limited.

If Larry had a chip on his shoulder, Archie certainly had chips on both of his. He could be very sarcastic, so it wasn't hard to fall out with him. He was also a bit high and mighty at times and wasn't the easiest person to get on with .... and he's still the same today. He palled about with Robbo and John McGovern but pretty much kept himself to himself.

I think Archie's best game was the 4-0 win over Manchester United. That night was Archie's night; he really stood out for me.

It's well documented what happened to him and Martin O'Neill before the European Cup Final when Cloughie left them both out. Archie was pissed off. He had missed out on the premier cup competition in the world and I suppose it ate away at him a bit.

The following season he was on his way to Birmingham. Martin stayed and played in the second game in the Berlin Stadium. The boss could have handled it better, but I'm sure he had his reasons. 8/10

John McGovern: A great skipper and a very important player. He is a big ACDC fan believe it or not and is very good on air guitar. Very under-rated. I don't think some of the fans realised the work he got through because he wasn't a spectacular player and had a bit of a funny way of running. He took a lot of stick but he didn't let it bother him. He just got on with things. He wasn't a spectacular player but he was very disciplined; he tackled honestly, sat in the middle, held it and then played a simple ball. He was a legend, another unsung hero. But he was useless at the toss up. Had a go at management at Bolton, but I think he was too nice and mild mannered for the job. 8/10

Ian Bowyer: I preferred him to Archie Gemmill in many ways. He was good fun. He could run for 90 minutes; he could tackle and he could also get you goals. He could also do a job at full-back if you wanted. Every side needs a 100% player like him. He will always be remembered for scoring one of the most important goals in the club's history. His header against Cologne was the turning point. A very under-rated player. 8/10

Martin O'Neill: The Squire was the hod carrier in the side. He did all the work and John Robertson got the praise. He would often go around in circles with two or three players around him and it drove Brian Clough to distraction. On one occasion he was asked to fill in for Viv and he said: "What am I, a dentist?"

Martin, an intelligent lad, was often at odds with the gaffer, who thought he was selfish. He was always second best to Robbo in the gaffer's eyes and had even considered going back to his law studies in Belfast.

And I don't think he ever quite got over being left out of the Malmo game, along with Archie, having played all the way to the final in 1979. I've heard it said that Cloughie hated Martin. I don't know about that. But he always had an opinion on something and the gaffer certainly didn't like that. He was on a hat-trick and buzzing in the Charity Shield game with Ipswich when Cloughie pulled him off. "Why did you do that?" asked Martin. "Because you're crap and you will always be crap" came the reply. Well, he did ask.

Martin wasn't crap, but he certainly wasn't as good as he thought he was. I think he was actually on the transfer list with Robbo when Cloughie arrived at the club. But he could do things no one else could do and did a lot of unselfish running, which perhaps some fans didn't appreciate. He was a vital cog and another unsung hero for me. He worked so hard for the team and had a good understanding with Viv. He was Brains, because he had one more GCSE than Rodney Trotter. He always came to training with a book and the Racing Post under his arm. He liked a bet now and again and even opened up a bookies with his brother in Nottingham. I'm not shocked   he has done so well as a manager. He did a magnificent job at Wycombe and went to Leicester at just the right time. But my missus could pick a Celtic team and I think his first real test is at Villa, but whatever the results, he will get the sack there, or walk away. 8/10

Peter Withe: Googie was a late starter, but he became a very good player. I played with him at Birmingham and Peter and Brian had obviously spotted his potential and snapped him up for a bargain £44,000. He was a big lad but he could run. He could also hold the ball up well. If it came down with snow on it he could control it on his chest – a bit like John O'Hare. He could turn a bad pass in to a good one. He could also score goals and, perhaps, never quite got the credit he deserved. He used to drive Peter and Brian mad when he flicked the ball on instead of holding it. Did well at a lot of clubs and won a European Cup medal with Villa. 8/10

Garry Birtles: He did well when he came in. He was third choice at one stage behind Steve Elliott before he injured his back. I think they got Garry from Long Eaton for a set of bibs and a few training balls; paid him five quid a week and sold him for a small fortune. Cloughie said that when he went to watch Garry play for Long Eaton the half-time drink was better than him. But he was a hard worker and I think he perhaps had more skills than Peter Withe. He quickly gelled with Tony Woodcock and it soon started to pay dividends. Like me, he liked a bet now and again. He ran for miles in games and used to take a lot of stick. But me, Larry and Ian Bowyer made sure we got them back. He struggled when he went to Man United; maybe it went to his head a wee bit. He has carved out a new career in the media and I'm delighted for him. 8/10

Tony Woodcock: He was a local lad who made good. He could have gone for a song at one stage because Brian Clough didn't think he was physical enough. Maybe he wasn't one of the most skilful at first but he caught on quickly and developed a knack of scoring goals. I've watched a few videos of him recently and he never gave defenders a minutes peace. He was an intelligent, quiet lad and did well for Arsenal and Cologne and won 40 caps for England. Always smartly dressed he was a bit fashion conscious. Always wore a tie. 9/10

John Robertson: My wee, tubby, scruffy mate. Liked his egg sandwiches, most of which used to drip onto his old desert boots, and a fag before games.

Robbo was a bit of a night owl. He liked his Brian Ferry records and knows every word Clint Eastwood ever spoke in a Dirty Harry film. He was very popular with the lads. He's a lovely fellow, what more can I say. I'm delighted that him and Martin O'Neill have been such a success at Leicester, Celtic and now Villa after starting off in the humble surroundings of Grantham and Shepshed. It just shows what can be achieved.

Robbo looked as though he should be selling the Big Issue (no disrespect to Big Issue sellers) but he was one of the best players I ever played with. I think, for three or four years, he was one of the best players in the world. His delivery was second to none. He was quality. He had so much belief in his own ability. He was pure magic when he had the ball at his feet. A very intelligent player, he could almost make the ball talk. The amount of games he played without getting injured was staggering for saying he had a target on his chest and defenders all over the world were queuing up to kick lumps out of him. Fortunately, he was that fat he didn't feel it. In five years he played 350 games and scored 90 goals. In one season alone he played in 79 games. Phenomenal. Teams had to double up to stop him, he was that good. Quite simply, he was the man that made Forest tick. Everything went through him and he was always capable of creating something out of nothing and making space for others. 10/10

John O'Hare: What a player. In his hey-day at Derby he was superb on that glue-pot of a pitch. He had so much skill up front and an amazing ability to kill the ball. Just kept it very, very simple. With Cloughie at Derby and Leeds, he was never going to be a first-team regular at Forest. But he could come in and do a job in midfield or centre-forward. A great mate, he would always be in my squad. I thought he would have made a good manager but he had a pub in Duffield for a while and then worked for Toyota. Scouts for Martin and Robbo at Villa these days. Great lad. Great squad player. 7/10.

Trevor Francis: He was the blue-eyed boy, Mr Golden Bollocks. He was also the bees-knees at Birmingham and cost Forest close to a record-breaking £1m. Talented, he could run at pace - Robbo never had that, he would just drop his shoulder and get the cross in. Some people might think I don't like Francis. But I never had a problem with him. I did perhaps envy him getting the headlines as the million-dollar-man. He could have a crap game and nick a goal and the national press would be raving about him. I also thought he was a bit of a diver, he sometimes went over far too easily.

I can't say I was ever close to him or that we were best mates, but I respected his ability. I was in the middle of my second wedding when I heard we had signed him. I think he bought a house with three acres of land at Little Carlton near Newark with six bedrooms, a swimming pool and indoor sauna. But he never phoned me to ask what Forest was like before he signed (mind you, I never spoke to Peter Withe before I signed). He didn't like wearing shinpads because they made his legs look bulky. But Cloughie said if he didn't wear them he wouldn't be playing. He wasn't a blood and thunder player and would never go for a 50/50 ball. And his pain barrier was just above his big toe.

Did well to come back from that Achilles tendon injury. But when I look back at him these days, I still do not regard him as one of the lads – even though he got the goal against Malmo that won the European Cup.

He might have thought he was something special, but he was just another player to me. Denis Law and Jim Baxter – now they were something special. 9/10

Stan Bowles: I was a shocked as anyone when Forest signed Stan. The gaffer liked hard workers and Stan certainly wasn't a worker. He didn't like travelling abroad and he also had a bit of a bad reputation as a gambler, drinker and womaniser. In fact, he made me look like Snow White. Not a Brian Clough type of player at all.

He wasn't an out-and-out goal scorer and that's what we needed at the time. He was an entertainer and provider. He used to go round in so many circles it's a wonder he didn't screw himself into the ground and come up with oil on his boots. He was a nice lad but in a fight with a fly, I'd back the fly every time. He is also the world's worst gambler. No matter where we were in the world he would find something to gamble on. When we played three card brag he would stick his hand in his top pocket and go £10 blind, £10 blind, then

£20. He'd end up owing the kitty £60 so I'd lend him £40 to carry on, so that's £100 quid he owes now. He ended up owing Martin O'Neill two grand when he left. I don't suppose Martin ever got it. We were going for a break in the sun but Stan, who was shit scared of flying, didn't turn up at the airport and missed the trip. He would have at least been on the bench for the European Cup final …. because we only had four subs that night.

Bryn Gunn: A nice local lad. I called him Bucket, because boy could he drink. Very dependable. Give him a job and he would do it.

Gary Mills: A nice looking, presentable young lad. He played for England youth at right-back, I believe. He was also pretty good at Rugby. Fit as a butcher's dog, he was an honest player who could run all day. Played the game the right way and he was a bit quick too. Could play in nearly every position. But you know what they say about a Jack of all trades don't you? Anyway, it's nice to see him doing well in non-League management since he retired.

Justin Fashanu: I think he was signed on the strength of one goal he scored for Norwich on Match of the Day. I'm told he was good at snooker, which is nice because he was crap at football. Held the club record for parking tickets and upsetting the gaffer, but that was about it. As the gaffer said, he couldn't trap a bus. Had to be the nicest smelling footballer in the world. It turned out that he was gay but we never even thought about it. He liked to make out he was a high-flyer, but he wasn't really. He lived in a bit of a dream world and said he talked to God. Cloughie famously had him arrested and escorted off the training ground. He should have done it sooner. But it wasn't Fash's fault the club paid so much money for him and I can't believe it was Cloughie who wanted to sign him.

Jimmy Gordon: I include the little Sgt Major because he was a vital member of the set-up at Forest. Jimmy was a great wee man who had been with gaffer at Derby. He was one of the few who would stand up to Brian. If something wasn't right he would tell him. He was the gaffer's eyes and ears and the gaffer listened to what he had to say. Took us for "training" most of the time. He was strict when we did train. I had a lot of respect for him.

Later Ron Fenton came in after being sacked by Notts County and he became BC's right-hand man. He was ok but I had a problem with him over training. I was cutting corners a bit and he accused me of cheating. "How am I cheating?" I asked. "You never said we couldn't cut corners. I was using my initiative so don't start picking on me you bandy-legged bad tempered bastard."

Proud to be skipper, but things didn't work out

My Elland Road error

The old Forest team was breaking up and I was playing centre-half alongside Bryn Gunn. I was ok but, to be honest, at the stage of my career, I wanted to get some money in the bank. I was getting a wee bit restless and I stood to get £25,000 for leaving the City Ground.

There were some good youngsters like Stevie Hodge, Colin Walsh, Chris Fairclough and Steve Chettle coming through and I just thought the writing was on the wall.

The gaffer obviously fancied Willie Young in place of me, although I didn't do myself any favours after getting banned for being sent off in a pre-season match in Spain. I tangled off the ball with Osasuna striker Iriquibal and got booked. Then I queried a decision and got my marching orders. Needless to say, the boss wasn't well pleased.

I asked for a move after a cup game. The boss asked me if I was sure and then got me to phone Willie Young to see if he fancied a move, just as I had done with Ian Wallace.

Before I knew it I was on the way to Leeds – bottom of the First Division - for £400,000. Man City had been interested but I only heard about Leeds' interest one morning before training and soon found myself signing a four-year contract after a brief meeting with Allan Clarke at the City Ground. It turned out to be a good bit of business for Forest - they made £250,000 profit on me – but it was one of the biggest mistakes of my career.

Just before I left I remember Peter Taylor asking "Are you sure?" Deep down I suppose I didn't want to go. I was obviously very sad to be leaving the City Ground. What we had achieved there was beyond my wildest dreams. It was a very strange feeling when I collected my things but, at my age, I had to look to the future. I was getting a £25,000 pay-off from Forest and I knew I could still do a job for somebody and I was, after all, still in Jock Stein's World Cup squad.

I never really bothered about contracts and it was all over pretty quickly. And, to be honest, I did not even know where Leeds were in the table. I knew they had decent players like goalkeeper John Lukic. He was a big, young, impressive keeper with good hands and played all 42 games in my first season.

And there was plenty of experience in the form of Paul Hart, Frank and Eddie Gray, Peter Barnes, a record £930,000 buy from West Brom, Derek Parlane and Trevor Cherry, but I didn't realise I was joining a struggling team.

I signed for £850 a week – the same as I was on at Forest, plus the offer of a club car.

I was shocked on my debut against West Brom when Clarke threw the ball at me and told me to lead the lads out. I was honoured, as one of the older players, to captain the club because I regarded them – when they boasted the likes, of Charlton, Madeley, Hunter, Bremner, Giles, Clarke and Lorrimer - as the best professional team I'd ever seen.

They could play football when they needed to. They could also kick when they had to. They had five or six players who could look after themselves and an astute manager in Don Revie – although he wasn't a patch on Brian Clough.

But I don't think my appointment went down too well with Cherry, who was big pals with Hart. I don't know if he knew about it, but if he didn't that was bad management. Whatever, it led to a bit of an atmosphere. I don't think it had anything to do with me coming from Forest, because Frank Gray had come back before me.

Leeds were still a big club with a fanatical fan base, but they had started the 1981-82 season disastrously, with only one win in ten games, when I arrived. They had leaked five against Swansea and four against both Coventry and Man City. I must have been a good luck omen because I made my home debut against West Brom and we won 3-1 and followed up by beating Sunderland 1-0 with a goal from Eddie Gray.

As luck would have it, the next game was at Forest. We lost 2-1. It was very, very strange going back that day. I got a tremendous reception from the crowd, I think there were over 25,000 packed in there. Leeds played well and were a bit unlucky not to come away with something. We lost 4-0 at Southampton – nothing went right for us that day – but one win in eight games after that really sealed our fate.

To make matters worse, I missed a couple of games through injury after hurting my hand in a freak accident in training. I went to grab hold of Peter Barnes' top just as he turned away and put my finger out. I had to go to hospital for an operation.

Clarke had a lot of faith in Barnes, who was a talented kid. But he was a bit lightweight and not the type of player who was going to dig you out of a hole. And let's face it, Leeds were sitting in a crater at the time.

Halfway through the season Frank Worthington was brought in to try and provide a few badly-needed goals. Now Frank had bags of experience and skill, to go with a brilliant football brain. He was an entertainer and crowd pleaser. But, like Barnes, he wasn't the man for a battle. He was a luxury player. We couldn't afford to carry one in the team, never mind two.

I was back for the home game with Liverpool, but we lost 2-0. We weren't disgraced and I think I went up front for a bit. Graeme Souness went over the top, fortunately I went a bit higher. He said I could have broken his leg. I said: "Better you than me." And we were Scottish team-mates at that.

We went six games without a win and that was the killer. Big Frank scored on his debut to give us a 1-0 win over Sunderland. He also scored in the 1-1 draw with Forest, from the penalty spot, and in the 2-1 defeat at Notts County. We beat Birmingham 1-0 away with a goal from Paul Hart, but it was a rare victory in what was fast becoming a disastrous season. As the pressure starts to build it affects your game. You whack it clear instead of trying to pass it for fear of giving a goal away. You are scared to make the mistake that might lead to the goal that relegates you.

I missed the games at West Ham and Villa through injury, but came on as sub in the 0-0 home draw with Stoke. I was back in the side for the game at Everton but we lost 1-0. We also lost at Spurs (1-2) and drew 3-3 with Birmingham, despite two goals from Frank Worthington, one from the penalty spot.

We then showed a bit of character to come back from behind to beat Brighton 2-1 through Hamson and Hird in an emotional game at Elland Road. It meant that we needed a point from our final game at West Brom to stay up. We lost 2-0.

The bottom line was that we just weren't good enough. It was a sad time. I had been brought in to shore up the back, but there is only so much one man can do. I don't blame myself; I gave it 100 per cent in every game. I really did.

Frank also did his bit with nine goals in 17 games but we finished 20th and were relegated from Division One. Inevitably, Clarke was sacked, even though he had been a hero at the club. Ok, he had not had the best of luck with injuries, but the simple fact was that there were too many 'average' players at the club.

Manny Cussins, the chairman, wasn't happy and took the club cars off me, Frankie Gray and Peter Barnes. I wasn't a happy man either, because although it wasn't written in the contract, we had a gentleman's agreement and that was good enough for me. I also didn't like the way Cussins disclosed details of my pay, which was £850 a week, £200 win bonus and £100 for a draw. That was no way for a gentleman to behave and no way to conduct the affairs of the club.

The problem with the car was eating away at me. Leeds had gone back on their word. They hadn't been honest and I wasn't having that. So I asked for a transfer.

When Clarke got the sack they made Eddie Gray MBE player-manager. Eddie may have impressed when coaching the kids, but he was too nice to be a manager. We used to pal about with Allan Clarke and go for meals at the Flying Pizza, which was superb.

I had the chance to go to Scunthorpe with Allan Clarke for £25,000 and there was also talk of a move to Coventry, but nothing came of it so I stayed where I was. I thought I could do better for myself.

But it got to the stage where I didn't want to play for Leeds after being relegated to the reserves. I went on strike I suppose. Eddie said he agreed with my stance – in principle. That was typical of Eddie, he was too nice for his own good, certainly too nice to be a manager.

To be a successful manager you have to be a lying, cheating bastard. Eddie certainly wasn't that. He was an honest man. I never really had a cross word with him and I can't say a bad word against him.

Leeds actually started the 1982-83 season in Division Two quite well without me. I was asked to sub at Fulham and we lost 3-2.

I wore the No4 shirt in the 2-1 home win over Cambridge and the 0-0 draw at Chelsea in front of a crowd of over 25,000.

Then I played in the 3-1 win over Burnley, the 0-0 draw at Blackburn and even managed a goal in the win over Newcastle at Elland Road. A crowd of 26,570 turned up to see Worthington and Butterworth complete a 3-1 success.

But things started to go wrong in November, which brought two defeats and two draws. December started with a 1-0 defeat at home to QPR and that was followed by four successive draws. We weren't losing many but two wins out of 16 wasn't good enough.

Worthington played his last game in the 0-0 draw with Middlesbrough as Gray gambled on promising youngsters. But one win from the last seven matches told its own story and Leeds finished 8th in the league with 60 points from 13 wins, 21 draws and only eight defeats.

Butterworth was top scorer with eleven goals. It was hardly the type of football to bring back the fans after relegation and I think the club plunged to over £2 million in debt at one stage.

I played 19 games in all that season, scoring twice, but when the offer came to rejoin Peter Taylor, on loan at Derby County, came along I jumped at the chance.

Paul Futcher and me defending against Plymouth Argyle at home in the FA Cup

Those Derby days

Derby offered me £600 a week and I was off. I knew Derby was a big club with a great history and the Baseball Ground was a great place to play. The atmosphere was brilliant. You were so close to the crowd that you could almost shake hands with them. The new stadium, nice as it is, does not have the same atmosphere.

But I only went to Derby because of Peter Taylor really. I wanted to help my old mate out. Plus, he said he would look after me.

Deep down, I was glad to get away from my nightmare at Leeds. I had a house at Collingham near Wetherby, but I suppose I had found it hard to settle in Yorkshire.

Peter also had his problems. There is an old saying about never going back to your old club, but Peter loved Derby. Simple as that.

Most of the time Peter was a joker and he could charm the birds out of the trees. But, once or twice at Derby, he got angry. He was a big chap, being an ex-goalkeeper, and it wasn't a pretty sight.

Money was tight, but it wasn't all bad news and he had inherited a few experienced players like Steve Powell, Steve Buckley and Dave Swindlehurst, along with a few decent kids, when he took over from John Newman.

The Rams also had big George Foster and John McAlle at the back and Bobby Davison and Kevin Wilson up front, good little workers who would also get their fair share of goals.

Steve Cherry, Gary Mills and Paul Hooks were also in the squad along with Paul Futcher, who went for a lot of money when he was a youngster. He was a quality player who should have done better but he never knew when to keep his mouth shut. He was always arguing with the manager. Swindlehurst was good at holding the ball up but he wasn't a patch on John O'Hare. He cost Derby a lot of money and never really repaid it. And, of course, there was little Archie…..

I can't say he welcomed me to the club with open arms. But that was Archie. He was a little scrapper but he was a hard man to like at times. He wasn't the most skilful of players but he had a great attitude and desire to win. Derby could have done with a couple more like him.

Peter said times were hard. For once, he wasn't joking. Although the club put me up at the Midland Hotel at first, they soon moved me out to the Kedleston Hotel. The hotel wanted the week's money in advance before they gave me a room, which shows you how far Derby's fortunes had fallen.

I was banned from driving at the time, so Kevin Wilson was my taxi driver. But Kevin, who ended up as manager of one of my old clubs, Ilkeston Town, was as good as gold and didn't seem to mind.

I had joined another club on the slide and we were certainly up against it. But, although I only played six games, I was never in a losing side and helped keep them up.

When I made my debut as a sub against Newcastle I flattened Kevin Keegan. As a result, the fans nicknamed me Yozza after the character from the Boys from the Black Stuff.

Even though I had played for Forest the fans soon took to me and I even managed a goal in the 1-1 home draw with Barnsley.....although I can't remember much about it. I missed the defeats at Blackburn and Palace but came back for the final match of the season at home to Fulham, which we won 1-0 thanks to a Davison goal. Derby finished 13th in Division Two and stayed up. Job done.

I went back to Leeds but got a phone call from Peter inviting me on the club trip to Magaluf. I shared a room with young Paul Hooks and we had a great time. We had some heavy drinking sessions and one night he fell over and knocked three teeth out, bang, clean as a whistle. He didn't realise until the next morning how bad it was. We tried to find him a dentist, but nothing could be done.

I was happy to stay at the Baseball Ground and I think Pete wanted to sign me on a permanent basis. But then Leeds called me back. I'd played less than half a season for them, 13 games in all and hadn't kicked a ball since March 12, but still got Player of the Year. I think that says it all. Nevertheless, it was an honour to follow in the footsteps of legends like Norman Hunter, Peter Lorimer, Allan Clarke, Mick Jones, Gordon McQueen, Tony Currie, Trevor Cherry and Eddie Gray. I missed the first six games, which produced two wins and three defeats. My return didn't improve things with successive defeats – 2-1 at home to Manchester City, 5-1 at Shrewsbury and 3-1 at Sheffield United with David Harvey, who had taken over from Lukic, between the sticks. He was a big, strong boy and wasn't a bad keeper either. But he was so laid back it was untrue. Nothing ever bothered him.

Martin Dickinson wore the No6 shirt. He was a local kid, not great on the ball, but at least he had a bit of pace.

We stopped the rot with three successive wins, Barnes even chipping in with a couple of goals, and a run of 1-1 draws against Palace, Blackburn, Derby and Chelsea. Sadly, that was followed by three successive defeats against Carlisle, Charlton and Huddersfield. I fell out with Gray's right-hand man Jimmy Lumsden and that was me done.

Things got so bad that Eddie told me to train by myself. In fact, I needn't even go in if I didn't feel like it. I kept myself fit in case someone came in for me. But I had to face facts, I was an outcast.

I thought about going to Seattle at one stage because there was money to be made in America. But it fell through in the end and I ended up back at Derby after making only 13 more appearances.

I was on £850 a week at Leeds and Peter Taylor said there was no way the Rams could match that, but I was that desperate to get away from Leeds and play regularly that I went back to Derby for £600.

By the time I returned, Peter had recruited Roy McFarland and Mick Jones from Bradford to help him – illegally as it happened - and done some wheeling and dealing. He'd got goalkeeper Jake Findlay on loan, but left him out after one game, while old hand Ray O'Brien came in from Notts County. Calvin Plummer, who'd been an apprentice at Forest was there along with big Dave Watson. The ex-England star was a good old warrior, with the heart of a lion, who had played all over the world.

And, of course, there was my old mate John Robertson…..

Brian Clough wasn't happy when Peter took the Derby job a few months after leaving Forest. But the signing of Robertson, while

Clough was walking the Pennine Way, caused a rift that was never healed.

I don't think Robbo really wanted to join Derby but he was sweet-talked by Peter into going. He cost Derby £135,000 but ended up going back to Forest for nothing. He could not wait to get away in the end.

I enjoyed playing alongside Watson, who was an England legend, even though I was having to play some games at full-back. He was a tough tackler and great header of the ball and was as hard as nails. I know because I ran into him once while he was playing for Manchester City. I don't recommend it. He nearly choked me. A great pro, he played to his strengths and kept it simple.

Derby were having a rough time by the time I got back. I think they lost seven out of eight and, to make matters worse, the Inland Revenue were chasing them for money.

Peter was sacked after we lost 5-1 to Barnsley. I don't suppose he could complain after such a bad run of results, but I think he had been let down by some of the players, who had formed little cliques. That just leads to friction and unrest. When you are in the shit the last thing you want is unrest; you all need to get stuck in and perform as a team.

The fans wanted Roy McFarland and he was put in charge with just nine games to save the club from relegation.

I never had a problem with Roy. There was talk that Clough and Taylor wanted to sign him to replace Larry and I would have loved to have had the chance to play alongside him. He was quality.

But Roy faced an impossible task. Although we beat Palace 3-0 with an Andy Garner hat-trick, we got slaughtered 4-0 at Newcastle and lost 3-0 at Shrewsbury in the last match of the season. Relegated.

I went on a golfing holiday after the last match and bumped into Henry Newton and Roy Mac, who told me that Arthur Cox had got the Derby job. Great!

I was used to the Clough and Taylor style whereas Cox was more like a Sgt Major, completely different. We started the season with Eric Steele in goal and Charlie Palmer and Steve Buckley at full-back. I was alongside big Floyd Streete and Stevie Powell. Arthur had also brought Kevin Taylor in from Sheffield Wednesday for £10,000.

Mickey Lewis arrived from West Brom. He looked like a tramp with football boots on. He even made Robbo look smart. His hair was like a bird's nest; he was all over the place. But he came in and did a good job. Cox also signed Steve Biggins, who had scored a lot of goals for Oxford, but he never quite made the step up, and splashed out big fees on Trevor Christie and Gary Micklewhite. All in all it was a far better team on paper than the season before.

It started well for me and Arthur asked me to be captain. The first game was at Bournemouth where I bumped into singer/actor Kenny Lynch, who I knew from celebrity golf days. "What are you doing down here?" he asked. Good question Ken. I was wondering that myself after we lost 1-0.

We hit back to beat Bolton 3-2 with a hat-trick from Kevin Wilson but lost 2-1 at Preston. We beat Lincoln 2-0 and the records show that I scored – but I can't for the life of me remember the goal.

The trouble with Arthur was that he was a workaholic and if he's in then you're in.

I was used to having a lot of free time but Arthur was a stickler for training. One day it had been snowing and there was slush all over the pavements. Instead of training in the warm in the gym at Raynesway, Arthur decided we were going on a run all the way up to Moorways.

It was crazy, not to mention dangerous. The players sent me, as skipper, to have a word and, let's say, it didn't go down too well.

From then on it was all downhill between Arthur and me and I found myself on loan at Notts County, who were managed by Richie Barker. I don't think I'd ever met Barker, who had played centre-forward for Clough and Taylor at Derby. I went because I just wanted to be playing football again …. and it was convenient.

Notts had been relegated under Larry Lloyd but had some good players like Rachid Harkouk, Paul Hooks, Steve Sims, Ian McParland and Pedro Richards, plus Dave Watson was there now. Mind you, so was Justin Fashanu. Although, to be fair, he did get eight goals for them. But I only played two games for Notts - a 2-0 defeat at Grimsby and a 0-0 draw with Oldham.

I was staying at Brailsford at the time and got snowed in for two games and then pulled a hamstring in a practice match. I was gutted.

Some players these days seem happy to sit on the bench and pick up their pay cheque every week. But not me. I was desperate to play.

When I went back to Derby, Arthur said: "How much do you want to go? I said 'the full amount, every penny', and he said "Ok."

Arthur Cox looked fearsome with his short hair. And he wasn't a man to cross. I remember him tearing a strip off goalkeeper Eric Steele after he heard him slagging a player off.

And once he challenged big Floyd to have a pop at him - if he thought he was hard enough. His head was about two inches from Floyd's nose. Wisely, Floyd never made a move.

So I suddenly found myself looking for another club again. I had an offer from Valetta in Malta, who were willing to pay me £200 a week.

It included accommodation for me and the family and six flights home a year. I'd had just about enough of this country so I said yes. I was due to fly out on the Tuesday when Allan Clarke phoned up and asked me to join him at Barnsley for £200 a week. I talked it over with the wife and I was suddenly on the way to Barnsley FC me duck, instead of Malta.

Allan, who was godfather to my daughter Laura, said he would look after me and asked me to take charge of the reserves. He said he would make sure that I wasn't out of pocket. I enjoyed it but I was spending a lot of time travelling up to training and sometimes, after a reserve match, I wasn't getting home until the early hours of the morning.

It was hard and tiring and to make matters worse, I never got any petrol money.

Clarke never really did me any favours and went back on his word. Matters came to a head after a reserve match when I tried to sub Billy Ronson, but he refused to come off. After the match I grabbed hold of the little shit and hung him on a peg in the dressing room.

The next day the gaffer called me in and asked me what had

happened. I told him and expected that Ronson would be fined and disciplined, but the next thing I heard he had been called into the first-team squad instead. So much for backing me up. There goes my authority.

I was choked because Allan and me were pals at Leeds and went on holiday together, but he let me down and I've never really spoken to him since. Honesty is a big thing with me and the bottom line was that he wasn't honest.

He said they could not afford me any more because they had been losing £3,000 a week since the miners' strike.

After that I was supposed to have signed for IF Elfsborg in Sweden. Forest manager Billy Davies said he met me over there once, but I don't remember setting foot in the country let alone playing for Elfsborg. No disrespect, but it sounds like a pint of lager to me.

So if anyone out there remembers me playing for Elfsborg, let me know…

My goal in the 1-1 draw with Barnsley

Peter Taylor and Roy McFarland reunited at the Baseball Ground

John Robertson runs out for Derby in a friendly at Meadow Lane

Richie Barker welcomes me on loan at Notts County

Justin Fashanu goes close for Notts against Oldham

Life in the non-League

I was still fairly young, but my legs had started to go a wee bit. I was never the quickest anyway, but I felt I could do a good job as a player-manager or manager. You don't play under the likes of Freddie Goodwin, Clough and Taylor and Arthur Cox without learning a thing or two, but I tried for a number of jobs without success.

So, in 1986, I decided to go part-time with Sutton Town with a great bloke called Bryan Chambers. He had a good reputation in local football, still does, and knows a lot of players. I loved it there and once rushed back from a business trip to Sweden to play at Harrogate. I got a taxi all the way back from Leeds airport. I wasn't getting paid, which meant I was well out of pocket.

But it was a friendly little family club and I thoroughly enjoyed my time there. I loved local football, because it was the grass roots. Without it there would be no Wayne Rooney or John Terry.

It was a good standard of football and we had some good players as well, like Phil Orton and keeper Mark Thornley. Martin Coupe was a good little player, who could certainly have performed on a higher stage. It was a good playing surface and I was happy jogging along on fifty quid a week. Unfortunately, the chairman Steve Cooke, from the Hardwick Motor Company, could not afford to keep the club going. It was a shame because he managed to keep my cars going. I was always banging them up, usually on the way back from the golf club after one shandy too many. I would take it to Sutton, borrow a courtesy car, and mine would be mended faster than Michael Schumacher's.

I had a full season there, and scored a few goals, before the money ran out and the players started leaving. It was a shame really because we would have easily won the league. I stayed on for half the money, but got booked a few times. Some were justified, others were just ridiculous. I think I was still a marked man as far as some referees were concerned.

After one game at Farsley Celtic we were starving and stopped off at an M1 service station in the mini-bus, which had no tax or MOT. It just so happened Forest were at Leeds that day and I was just tucking into a couple of hamburgers when Cloughie walked by. "Ok Kenny," he said, looking at the two bits of charred meat in my hand. "They're no mine," I said. "I'm minding them for a friend."

I polished them off as soon as his back was turned. After all we got three points that day and they'd got sod all at Leeds. I reckoned I'd earned them.

When Bryan Chambers went to Stafford Rangers he asked me to go pre-season training with them. We had to run up a hill, it was hellish. To make matters worse a television crew turned up to film me and I was dying on my feet. This young guy with a camera the size of a shed was running up the hill backwards and he was still going faster then me.

The fact was I just couldn't get round the pitch any more. I had the chance to go to Shepshed but I thought - sod that.

The years were catching up with me faster than most so I quit to run a pub out in the sticks, the Blacksmiths Arms at Marchington, with my second wife, Louise. It's amazing how many footballers go into pubs when they pack up. Robbo had one at Aslockton. In our day many footballers didn't know what else to do. Few had an education to fall back on all they did was train, play football, have a good time and go home. Many just weren't prepared for a life outside football.

I'd hooked up with Louise after splitting up with my first wife, Pat. She was four years younger than Pat and she turned out to be a right bitch. I was warned that she was just a gold digger, but I didn't listen.

Now I know what you are thinking. Kenny Burns in a pub. But I had a rule that I wouldn't drink until after ten at night. If a regular bought me a drink, I'd stick to a half just to be sociable – although I did get a taste for that Burton beer.

Now I had never been any good with money and I lost money in the pub, it was too far off the beaten track and only two customers ever walked there.

But I really enjoyed the pub life. It was a lovely spot, with brasses, horse-shoes and all that stuff. I was especially nice when there was a log fire blazing in winter, and we even started serving meals. But the local farmers didn't know me from Adam. All they talked about was how long it took to dip a sheep and the price of hay.

I even started a darts team with the best players from Burton and Uttoxeter and we used to put chips on and bread and dripping. It went down a storm.

The trouble was, we had to make £365 a week just to cover the rent alone and that was before paying for the light and everything else.

It was hard work and it led to rows with the wife. She eventually moved into a house with our two girls, Laura and Emma. I said she could take some furniture for the house, but when I got back from a game at Wolves she had almost cleaned me out. All that was left was a television, a chair and a bed. It was the beginning of the end of my career as a publican.

One day I got a call from Robbo asking me to join him and Martin O'Neill at Grantham for £60 a week. That was a nice little club as well and it was great to team up with the lads again. We had a few laughs that season but it took me well over an hour to drive there so I didn't train.

According to one book I've seen on Forest players, I then went to Gainsborough Trinity as player-coach, followed by Oakham. It's news to me. I don't even know where Gainsborough is and I certainly don't remember being player-coach at Oakham.

In July 1989, I signed for Ilkeston Town, who were managed by Carl Francis and former Sutton Town boss Steve Giles. I was his first signing since he took over from Denis Jenas.

I met the chairman, Paul Millership, for talks at the Post House in Sandiacre. He offered me £60 a week and a job at Manor House Furnishings, which suited me at the time.

Millership was a self-made man and he liked a drink. Money was nothing to him at the time and he picked out a new car for me. Very nice.

I hadn't done anything like this before but I think I was quite a good salesman. Why? I had the gift of the gab – ok I was a gobby bastard – but, above all, I was honest. Honesty is always the best policy. I made my debut at Long Eaton in a Midlands League Supreme fixture and scored my first goal for the club the following month in the FA Cup at Colwyn Bay.

The old Manor Ground, which now has a supermarket on it, had a sloping pitch and I had to wait until November for my first goal there, scoring twice against Melton Town. In all, I played 38 games that season, hitting the target eleven times.

I was getting my fair share of goals but things were not going very well for us at the Old Manor ground. Francis was sacked and Bill Fossey came in along with his son-in-law, David Beavon. I didn't rate Fossey, we just didn't see eye to eye. I stood in midfield and passed the ball on. He wanted more out of me, but I was 35 and couldn't run around the pitch any more.

I suppose I also resented someone like Fossey telling me, a former European Cup star, how to play football and it wasn't long before we fell out over my disciplinary record.

I got sent off in the 3-2 defeat at Wednesfield – our first in 17 games – and he threatened to strip me of the captaincy. We were leading 1-0 when I got my marching orders along with one of their players. But I can understand why he was upset – after all I had only just come back from a three-match suspension.

I was top scorer with 20 goals in 35 appearances and showed I still had a bit to offer with two hat-tricks. I got all the goals in a 3-1 win over Wednesfield and got the second in the home win over Tividale in the West Midlands Regional League, Premier Division – the club had been demoted because there were no floodlights.

One of the best games I played in was the superb 5-1 FA Cup win over Grantham on their impressive new ground in August 1991. Robbo was in charge then and when the fifth went in he shouted "For fucks sake, Burnsie haven't you got enough?"

We lost only one League game that season ….and I wasn't playing that day.

One of the toughest games I played in was against the Police at the old Manor Ground. We had only just kicked off when the Police centre-half smashed our winger into the fence. A couple of other tackles soon went flying in. Talk about the long arm of the law - they were getting away with murder.

Fortunately, we had a player called Nigel Gillott, who was a bit handy. He could play a bit as well. On this occasion he went into a tackle with their centre-half who came out with a split eye.

In one game at Leigh RMI our striker, Steve Culley was dumped on his backside every time he got the ball. He was kicked black and blue and we had to take him off in the end. We went 1-0 down and I was pushed up front to try and grab a goal. But I ended up grabbing their centre-half instead and left him spread-eagled in the box. That one was for Steve.

I actually played in the last ever game at the old ground, opening the scoring in the 4-0 win over Great Wryley, taking my total for the season to 19. I also played in the 4-1 win over Cannock Chase as we clinched a League and Cup double.

Things came to a head with Bill Fossey after a training session at Shipley Park. We used to give a yellow jersey to the worst trainer and on this occasion Bill tripped over the ball and rolled down the hill. The lads all fell about laughing so I presented him with the yellow jersey. It was just a bit of fun, but he took it the wrong way. He thought I was taking the piss out of him and undermining his authority. I wasn't. As I said, it was just a bit of fun.

That's one thing about local football. You can have a right laugh, as long as you don't take it too seriously. This is how daft referees can be. In one match Stevie Giles ran onto the pitch with the magic sponge to treat a player. The ref asked him his name and he said 'Mickey Mouse'. The ref said "I'm booking you for coming onto the field of play without permission Mr Mouse." I think Steve got fined £50 for that.

I used to give little Vince Duffy some stick and I was always rowing with a lad called Kevin Leame. Every time he'd try and get a bit intellectual with me I'd just say: 'Two European Cups, piss off'. Game set and match to me.

When Fossey eventually resigned, I thought I would get the job – I really fancied it - but Millership never mentioned it. I didn't press it and Danny Boyes was put in charge. Danny wanted me to help some of the young, inexperienced players and put me back to centre-half alongside Johnny Humphries. We did ok and I scored a screamer against Dunkirk. Not bad for an old, fat lad.

I played in the first game at the New Manor Ground, against Chasetown in August 1992 and made my last appearance that November – a 5-0 defeat at Paget Rangers.

I was missing training and Danny Boyes fined me. Eventually he dropped me to give a young lad called Carl Thomas a game.

It didn't go down too well with Millership, or me, for that matter. The chairman wanted a big name in the side to help put bums on seats. Although I'm told that gates doubled after I left!

As a double European Cup winner I didn't like being left out, but perhaps it was time to move on again. I had scored 55 goals in 124 appearances, not bad considering I played a lot of games in defence and midfield.

I enjoyed my time at Ilkeston - it's a hot-bed of football situated as it is between Derby and Nottingham - and made many friends over there. In fact, I'm still in contact with a lot of them.

I also enjoyed playing with the Vets side under Danny Boyes and Tony Smith. I don't think we lost in the two years I was there.

When Danny rang and asked me if I was interested in playing I was tempted to say "Piss off." But they had some good players like Steve Culley, little Vince Duffy (who I'm told used to clean my boots at Forest) and the Harbottle brothers, Dave and Mark, who could both play a bit.

I remember one game against West Brom who had my old adversary, John Wile playing. I turned the clock back a bit with a towering header into the top corner, but we almost never got to the match. The bus driver got lost so I took over as navigator, having played for Birmingham I knew my around didn't I? Unfortunately, I took us the wrong way down a one-way street and almost started a riot among the locals.

In another match at Wolves, we came up against Phil Parkes, Steve Daley and Mel Eves and won 5-1, I think

We even got to Wembley one year. It was the warm up match before the Manchester United v Arsenal Charity Shield game.

We booked into a nice hotel in London and it didn't take me long to empty the mini bar. That gave me an appetite, so off I went for a curry. I went back to the hotel for a few more drinks and then someone suggested we went for another curry. Nice.

We were up against Billingham Strollers, who took it so seriously that they even flew in a player who had been with Ajax. But the match itself was a bit of a farce. I think we played 20 minutes in the first half and ten in the second and lost 1-0 with the Arsenal and United players looking on. Still, it left more time for drinking. As usual, I got pissed.

There was trouble one year at the club's Christmas do and, for once, I wasn't involved. We all met up at a bar in Hockley carrying our club tracksuits – for some reason Fossey wanted them handing in that night. We then went for a meal at the Cricketers, which boasted a Chinese restaurant at the time. The waiter came out, took one look at me and then ran straight back into the kitchen. I thought bloody hell what have I done now? But he came out a few minutes later with a big photograph for me to sign.

After a few drinks we went to the Palais and Bill Fossey split his silver suit doing the twist, which had all the lads in hysterics. Apart from a young lad called Steve, who was drowning his sorrows after being released by Notts County.

He was a bit the worse for wear so Danny Boyes and Shane Guyatt put him in a taxi. Unfortunately he was sick all over the place. There was a bit of a rumpus and Danny ended up going to hospital for treatment on a cut hand. The police arrested him, even though he was only trying to defend himself.

We all went round the nick to try and get him out but they kept him until the next morning. Just another typical lads night out at Ilkeston Town. There was never a dull moment.

I had three good years at Ilkeston. I just stood in midfield in the end and pinged it about. Like Cloughie said, let the ball do the work!

Sadly, I didn't have much luck with the company cars. I was supposed to be going to Gibraltar to play in an old boys game after a match at Gresley. But I had a cold coming and went on the brandy, just for medicinal reasons you understand. Well, after about fifteen or so, I was well medicinal. The lads told me not to drive and tried to take the keys off me, but I didn't listen. The next thing I knew the car was nose down on a bowling green. I say ON, but it was more like wedged IN the bowling green.

I phoned the missus and got my golf clubs out of the car and lay on the grass until she picked me up. The next day I went to Gibraltar hoping it would all blow over, but when I got back the chairman was on the phone. The car had been reported stolen, so I got away with that one.

Understandably, the chairman was reluctant to give me another car, but I got one in the end.

Unfortunately, I had a few too many one night at the golf club. I'd split up with the missus and was drinking far too much. The car knew it's own way home from the golf club but on this occasion it missed the turn for home and I ended up ploughing into a tree. The car was a right mess and so was I. This time I phoned a friend who took me back to his house. Once again, I got away with it.

No wonder my relationship with the chairman went downhill rapidly after that. I used to play golf and snooker with him. If you were his pal he was as good as gold.

One night we went to a local chip shop and he bought a load of chips, pies and fish and took them to the factory where some of the girls were doing overtime on a rush order that had to be ready for the next morning.

He had a couple of companies and brought a lot of employment to Ilkeston. But if you got on the wrong side of him he could be a right bastard. He would bellow "If you don't want to work, piss off."

It didn't matter if it was a man or a woman. He didn't have a problem with that. He could be a nasty bit of work, but he got the job done.

I was on shit money but I had to put up with it because I didn't know where the next wage packet was coming from. I eventually lost my job. I can't complain, it was my own fault. I was still drinking too much, mostly at night for something to do.

So now I had no job, no car, no money coming in and, worst of all, no football. Things got so bad that I ended up on the dole. I was sleeping a bit rough and was too embarrassed to go in and sign so I gave them the address of a friend in Brailsford, who offered to put me up for a while.

I'd won two League Cups, two European Cups and was Footballer of the Year. But that hardly qualified me to drive a forklift truck, did it?

It was a very, very sad time and I was at a low ebb, although there were people worse off than me I suppose.

I believe that before anyone can help you, you have to help yourself, so I decided to get away and moved into the Clovelly hotel near Derby. I got a special deal of £40 a week if I looked after my own room.

I had a job as a rep for a gift-wear firm in Southwell owned by a Forest fan, Ian Guise, for while and did ok until I lost my licence again. He took me out to China to see the factories where the goods were made and that was a real eye opener. You were travelling up dirt tracks to these "factories" which were usually in very poor areas. He used to ship stuff like cast iron doorstops and clocks – of all shapes and sizes – over by the container load because it was so cheap to make them out there.

I enjoyed selling and I think the customers, at places like garden centres and Bennetts in Derby, liked me because I told them the truth. I would walk in to a new client and break the ice by saying "What comes after S?" They would answer "T" and I would say "Two sugars please." I used to make up a couple of fictitious calls and, with a bit of luck, I could be on the golf course in the afternoon getting my handicap down to seven.

Then the chance to work on the radio came along and I can't thank Darren Fletcher, who is on Five Live these days, enough for that. They were looking for someone to work alongside Garry Birtles who took over when Larry Lloyd was ditched for upsetting David Platt. Larry wasn't too happy and felt Garry had gone behind his back. What did he expect Garry to do? Turn work down?

It kept me occupied two or three days a week. I used to get a bus from Derby to the Broad Marsh and walk up to the radio station. I'd got my swagger back. I felt like an important person again. I was back on the map. My last club in football was Telford. My pal Gerry Daly was manager there and asked me to give him a hand. I don't know what he was doing there because he hated football. He claimed he was a penalty king – burger king more like. He'd rather be playing snooker than football even though he got 46 caps with the Republic of Ireland. I tried my best to bring a wee bit of professionalism to the club; to teach them the good habits I had learned at Forest under Clough & Taylor, but it didn't really work out.

I played one or two charity games, one for television actor Robert Lindsey at Ilkeston, but that was it.

I also played in the match to raise funds for cash-strapped Notts County and it nearly killed me. I could not walk for a week after that and then I found out that Notts had been saved any way. I needn't have bothered!

It was shame when the radio show finished because we had built up quite a following. I was at a loose end now and had to find something to do. Les Bradd invited me to work for Forest on match days and I loved it. I hadn't seen much of Forest in the Stuart Pearce era, but it was a great feeling just to walk into the City Ground again.

Back to the grass roots at Sutton Town

Sutton Town: Back, from left, B Chambers (manager), J Swinbourne, S Lamb, D Burrows, M Thornley, M Jones, P Baker, A Humphries. Front, A Kirk, K Burns, N Lovell, M Laverick, M Richardson, M Coupe, P Milnes.

Ilkeston Town: Back, from left, S Giles, T Cuthbert, K Burns, P Naylor, K Shaw, S Wiggins, N Gillott, S Cockayne, C Francis. Front, P Baker, P Ingle, D Price, D Markham, D Taylor, K Ward, I Baggeley

King of the old Manor Ground

Left: Still got a bit left in the tank, but not much. Right: Final game at the Manor Ground. Keeper Alan Rigby and club president Robert Lindsay admire my hairstyle

Television all-stars charity match. Standing, from left, T Williams, B Price, G Craven, F Hines, P Greenwood, R Cook, K Burns, R Harper, P Duncan. Front, D Jenson, R Lindsay, T Selby, T Osoba, R North. Front: R Askwith

Back in a Forest shirt and playing for Ilkeston Town

Back at Wembley with Ilkeston Town vets

Kicking off at Wembley watched by Manchester United and Arsenal players

Ilkeston Town FC under Bill Fossey. We had some good players like Dave Charlesworth, Larry Burrell, Alan Rigby and Tony Reid, who had been on Derby County's books.

A proud Scot. It meant a lot to me just standing there

Scotland the brave

Let me say from the off that I'm very proud to be Scottish. It's bred into you. And I love Scotland, it's a great country – although, I have to admit, just like England there are some shitty bits and there were a few arse holes I couldn't get on with.

But I never felt completely accepted in the national team. Maybe it's that Anglo-Scottish divide. I don't really know. Anyway, I don't think I felt at home when I played for Scotland.

The Scottish Press always seemed to favour the whole-hearted home-based players like Tom Forsyth. I was proud to play for my country, of course I was. But to me it was just another game. It was part of my job.

I'll always be grateful to Andy Roxborough, who gave me my chance for the youth team, along with Frank Gray, when we beat England 1-0 at Villa Park.

And I'll never forget when we played a tournament in Switzerland, that was a great experience.

We lost our first game in Basle and were a bit dejected. But then we got to wear a white kit with red socks. Great. For 90 minutes we thought we were like Real Madrid. I think I managed to score two goals but England, who we had already beaten, won the tournament. We were a wee bit peeved to say the least.

I started to make a name for myself after scoring four goals for the Scottish professional youth team in the UEFA tournament in Barcelona in 1972. I also got booked – as usual. But I was trying to mend my ways…honest! Although we beat West Germany 1-0 and Russia 2-0, the Germans went through on goal difference because we lost the first game to Hungary 4-3.

My mate, Jim Cannon, was sent off in the game against Russia in Jativa, which didn't help our chances. We already had to win by four clear goals on a hard, bumpy pitch to overtake section winners West Germany, who had beaten Hungary 3-2. I gave us the lead a minute before half-time when I hammered in a cross from Dunfermline's Jim

Scott, who made it 2-0 after 61. Then the referee gave a controversial penalty but Leeds keeper Jon Shaw made a great save.

I played for the Professional Youth X1 against the Scotland U-23 side, who included Alan Rough, Gordon McQueen, Willie Young, Jim Bone and Lou Macari and I scored a beauty in the 5-2 defeat at Firhill. Celtic's Brian McLaughlin hit a long ball and I held off two challenges before lobbing the advancing Rough. Doug McLachlan, who was with Preston, got the other.

We did ok for saying we were all under 18 and only conceded a few near the end when we started to tire. I was happy with my goal, considering I had played for Birmingham the previous night.

Tommy Docherty, who had signed a four-year contract to be Scotland boss before the game, was impressed by my display and tipped me for great things in the future.

The Doc also saw me score for Scotland Professional Youths in a friendly against Ross County at Victoria Park, which only had a small 250-seat stand. I think he was there to switch on the new floodlights at Dingwall. We edged a seven-goal thriller and I scored in the 80th minute with a well-placed header.

I also played two U-23 games while I was at Birmingham. I made my debut in a 3-0 win against Wales in Aberdeen in 1974 and the 2-0 defeat in Holland two years later. The likes of Graeme Souness, Billy Bremner and Kenny Dalglish were in the team. For me, Dalglish was up there with the best to have ever pulled on the famous blue shirt and that includes Law, Baxter and Jimmy Johnstone.

I also liked Chelsea star Charlie Cooke, but he was coming towards the end of his international career when I saw him. For a winger, he had every attribute. Skill wise he had the lot and could also score goals. Danny McGrain was also a good player – but I'd rather have Viv Anderson in my team any day.

Big Joe Jordan put himself about and roughed defenders up. But I have seen better headers of the ball. Like Joe, Gordon McQueen had a presence, he was a big lad but he could motor once he built up a head of steam.

Don Masson, who was such a big cheese at Notts County, got into the Scotland side. He was a quiet player and he only loaned you the ball. He wanted to take every free-kick, penalty and throw-in. When he passed it, he wanted it straight back. He runs a B&B near Nottingham these days.

Tommy Docherty called me up to the full squad for the first time in December 1972, after the Little World Cup. I was only 18 at the time and had only played half-a-dozen League games at Birmingham. They were all in midfield – even though I had a fine goalscoring record for the Reserves.

Suddenly I felt six feet tall. I was certainly proud to be Scottish that day.

The Doc was a bubbling character, always laughing and joking and you played with a smile on your face under him. Things were never the same under Willie Ormond after the Doc resigned to take over at Manchester United.

It was Ormond, who died at the age of 57, who actually gave me my debut in West Germany in 1974. I was playing alongside David Hay, Kenny Dalglish, Denis Law, Willie Morgan and Martin Buchan.

I was looking forward to playing at the back but they gave me a holding role in midfield – against Beckenbauer and co. Thanks very much for that.

It didn't take me too long to realise that I was completely out of my depth. I was left chasing shadows. Germany were just different class, I couldn't even get close enough to them to kick them and it was a relief when I was taken off because I was blowing out of my arse. We lost 2-1, despite a goal from Dalglish. They had a superb side and ran us ragged from the first minute until the last.

Denis Law was the first to congratulate me on my debut and that's something I will never forget. It meant a lot to me because I think that was his last game for Scotland.

Law was a hero that side of the border. Before the 1986 World Cup I was invited to Scotland with him and we stayed in a plush hotel. I was lying on the bed drinking some wine when the phone went. It was Denis wanting to know if I fancied going out for a drink. I actually stood up. When Denis Law invites you out for a drink you don't say no.

We got a taxi and everywhere we went he was treated like a god, it was unbelievable. The man had an aura about him. He was very, very special.

I made my full home debut for Scotland against East Germany. I came on when the indestructible Jim Holton was carried off after bad foul, and scored in a 3-0 win. The ball came to me at the back post about a yard out, just the way I like them and I smashed it into the opposite corner. I was nervous and I think I miss-hit it a bit but it went in and that's all that counts.

It was a memorable moment and one I still cherish. We got two penalties that day but big Joe Jordan missed one. We got paid £100 I think, but I would have played for nothing. It was the first time Scotland had scored three goals at Hampden in over five years.

My next game was the 2-1 defeat by Spain in front of over 92,000 at Hampden. It was all a bit of a blur, but Bremner, who was captaining the side, got the goal. It was unbelievable playing at Hampden Park. It's a very, very special place. When you ran onto the pitch you could cut the tension with a knife. But the roar from the crowd! That's something you never forget. It still sends tingles down the spine just thinking about it. It was the same on the trips back from Largs into Glasgow. The fans would come out in their thousands to cheer us. It was unbelievable.

I only played once the following year and was subbed 15 minutes from time by Paul Wilson in the 1-1 draw with Spain in Valencia. It was his only appearance in a Scotland shirt.

We took the lead in the first minute when Charlie Cooke's superb pass led to a headed goal from Jordan. Spain's equaliser was controversial. The referee gave a penalty after Martin Buchan handled on the line, but changed his mind and gave a goal instead.

I played twice in 1976. The first game, a World Cup qualifier away to European champions Czechoslovakia in Prague, was a disaster and ended in a 2-0 defeat – our first in nine games.

We started well enough with Andy Gray and Joe Jordan playing in front of a midfield of Rioch, Dalglish, Masson and Gemmill.

But, a minute after the break, Rough parried a shot and Panenka smashed in the loose ball. Two minutes later impressive winger Petras got the second. To make matters worse, Andy Gray was sent off on his debut on foreign soil for retaliation against Ondorus. Gemmill, who was captaining the side, McQueen, Buchan and Donachie were all booked as the tackles started to fly in. Although we were forced to field a weakened team against Wales a month later, we managed a 1-0 win after a back heel from Dalglish was deflected in by Crystal Palace defender Ian Evans.

A number of players suddenly pulled out ahead of the game with Sweden at Hampden, so Asa Hartford and Willie Johnston were recalled from the wilderness. Asa scored with a long-range shot that went in via a post and the keeper's back. Dalglish also scored with the help of the woodwork.

Sub Joe Craig, who replaced me, got the other with his first touch in international football – a header. Ormond resigned before the game with Wales at Hampden to join Hearts and Ally MacLeod came in. Ormond had been unsettled by rumours of Jock Stein getting his job and decided to jump ship back to his council house in Mussleburgh. But Stein, recovering from a car crash, was under contract to Celtic. In the end, it was MacLeod who got the nod.

He made Bruce Rioch skipper for the 0-0 draw with Wales – the first English-born player to captain Scotland. I don't know if it was popular with the fans but I didn't have a problem with Bruce being skipper.

I missed the next nine games but came on as sub in the 1-1 Home International draw with Northern Ireland, on May 13, in place of Martin Buchan. MacLeod, with the World Cup in mind, experimented with two big men in attack, Joe Jordan and Derek Johnstone. John Robertson, on his debut, was to supply them with the ammunition, but it was Bruce Rioch who cut the ball back for Johnstone to head the equaliser in the 40th minute.

Martin O'Neill had given Northern Ireland (who were forced to play all their games away from home because of the political situation) the lead after 26 minutes.

Three days later Johnstone also scored with a brilliant header in the 1-1 draw with Wales at Hampden. I replaced Buchan and Robbo dropped to the bench. We took the lead after only 12 minutes with a brilliant goal. Souness and Dalglish combined to send Gemmill free on the right and Johnstone met his cross with a stunning diving header.

Brian Flynn hit the post with a penalty after Tom Forsyth had handled, before Willie Donachie rolled the ball past Jim Blyth for the softest of own goals in the 91st minute. To make matters worse Gordon McQueen injured his knee after crashing into a post.

I kept my place for the big one, the game against England on May 20, which attracted a crowd of over 83,000. Joe Jordan was recalled even though he had only scored twice in four years for Scotland, while Souness and Gemmill made way for Rioch and Masson. Francis was in the England team along with Dave Watson.

We had most of the play but lost 1-0 to a late Steve Coppell goal after Rough was "nudged" by Peter Barnes. The game was ruined by a whistle-happy French referee. He blew for every bit of physical contact – apart from the kick-off when Bruce Rioch and Emlyn Hughes shook hands.

The crowd were magnificent that day, you would have thought judging by the Hampden Roar that we had won not England.

I was in the squad for the 1978 World Cup finals after we finished top of the qualifying group, which include Czechoslovakia and Wales.

The 22 were: Goalkeepers: Alan Rough (Partick), Bobby Clark (Aberdeen), Jim Blyth (Coventry).

Defenders: Sandy Jardine, Tom Forsyth (Rangers), Martin Buchan, Gordon McQueen (Man Utd), Willie Donachie (Man City), Kenny Burns (Nottm Forest).

Midfield: Don Masson, Bruce Rioch (Derby County), Archie Gemmill (Nottm Forest), Asa Hartford (Man City), Lou Macari (Man Utd), Graeme Souness (Liverpool).

Forwards: Joe Jordan (Man Utd), Derek Johnstone (Rangers), Kenny Dalglish (Liverpool), Joe Harper (Aberdeen), Willie Johnston (West Brom), John Robertson (Nottm Forest).

We were 8-1 with the bookies to lift the trophy, but we were without the injured Gordon McQueen and Danny McGrain. Willie Donachie was suspended and Andy Gray was surprisingly ignored. Amazingly, over 25,000 fans turned up just to see us off. They paid

50p just to see us ride round Hampden Park on open-top lorries and they sang and cheered their heads off. Amazing.

Sadly it all went horribly wrong after that. We lost 3-1 to Peru, after Alan Rough got beaten twice at his near post. Joe Jordan gave us the lead when their keeper could only turn away a Bruce Rioch shot, but Peru equalised three minutes before the break when Cuerto beat Rough.

Don Masson had a tame penalty saved at 1-1 after Cubillas was harshly ruled to have fouled Rioch. It should have been re-taken because the keeper definitely moved early. I couldn't pronounce the names of any of the Peru team and the manager told us not to worry about them because they were a team of old men. But, as it turned out, they weren't mugs.

They had a world-class player in the veteran Teofilo Cubillas, who hit two goals in the last 20 minutes, while Oblitas and Munante gave the inexperienced full-backs a torrid time.

MacLeod should have made changes because Rioch and Masson could not cope, but he didn't have a clue what to do. When he finally sent on Gemmill and Macari in place of Masson and Rioch it was too late.

Willie Johnston was supposed to be the key man for us, getting balls in for Jordan and Dalglish but he failed to make an impact in what was a very poor display all round.

John Roberston replaced Willie Johnston for the second game against Iran and MacLeod paired me with Martin Buchan, even though we had never played together before, in the centre of defence. Willie Donachie was back after suspension and Gemmill and Macari replaced Masson and Rioch.

There was still no place for Souness and Derek Johnstone and the result was a 1-1 draw. We got the boost of an unusual own goal two minutes before the break and should have killed them off. The turning point came when we lost Buchan, who cut his head in a collision with Donachie. MacLeod played safe by replacing him with Forsyth, but 13 minutes from time, disaster struck when Danaifar held off Gemmill and beat Rough from an acute angle.   We had to gamble now to stay in the tournament but what did MacLeod do? He sent on little Joe Harper in place of Dalglish with 15 minutes to go. It was a shambles and left us needing to beat Holland by at least three goals.

It was rough on the loyal Scotland fans who had made 7,000-mile journey out to Argentina and I can understand why some yelled abuse as we trooped off.

I was dropped ahead of the famous victory over Holland. Robbo was also left out as Graeme Souness, Kennedy and Forsyth came in. I blame Archie Gemmill for getting me axed, but I suppose he did go out and score one of the best goals in the history of the competition, as well as a penalty, as Scotland won 3-2. But it wasn't enough. Peru had beaten Iran 4-1 with a hat-trick from Cubillas. We went out on goal difference and Holland went on to the final.

Alan Rough let some bad goals in. He wasn't the only one to blame, but it is criminal for a keeper to be beaten at his near post. In any event, we were out and on the way home.

It wasn't a great trip all round from the start. The officials' bus ahead of us broke down on the way to the hotel in Cordoba and our bus had to push it up the hill. We ended up carrying our suitcases up the hill to the hotel, which was next to a casino.

When we nipped over the fence to have a look at the casino we were surrounded by armed guards.

The hotel was a bit of a dump and was still being decorated, but there was the luxury of a swimming pool. Unfortunately, it was full of rubbish and Martin Buchan spoke for us all when he said: "I'm not staying in this shit-hole."

Now, I would have stayed in a tent if it meant playing for Scotland but it has to be said that this was only two star accommodation at best – and that's being generous.

The insects drove you mad, the rooms were very basic and, although the food was ok, it was nothing special. At least they had the Two Ronnies and Morecambe & Wise on in the television. room, so it wasn't all bad news.

Just for good measure, the so-called training pitch was hard and rutted and there was trouble brewing in the squad over bonuses.

To make matters worse the press were blowing the slightest

incident out of all proportion. There were stories of boozing, gambling and loose women – most of them untrue. Not the best preparation for a World Cup campaign then.

Now I know the Scots have a reputation for being a bit tight, but you would think that, for the World Cup, the Scottish FA would have fixed us up with something better than that. The organisation was very poor to say the least.

The biggest news, I suppose, was when Willie Johnston was sent home after the Peru game for taking drugs, usually prescribed for mental and physical fatigue. He got slaughtered in the Press. Now, we were mates but he never said anything to me about taking drugs and I never suspected. Lots of players used to take "sleepers" in those days so that good a good nights kip before big games.

It was a sad trip home. At the end of the day we had failed. We had let the country, and ourselves, down.

Jock Stein replaced MacLeod when he left to manage Ayr United. My first game under him was the vital European Championship game in Norway, which we won 4-0. I was planning to go on holiday until my golf partner said he had seen my name in the Scotland squad that morning. I telephoned my brother in Glasgow and he looked it up in Scottish Sunday newspaper.

My big mate, Ron Hulme, laid on a car for me and made a made dash to Glasgow to meet up with the team.

I don't know what had gone wrong. But I hadn't heard from Stein and neither had Forest. I knew Archie and Robbo were in the squad and had wished them all the best after our European Cup celebration.

Archie Gemmill captained the side but was dropped for the 1-1 draw with Peru. Again we should have beaten them, but this time John Wark missed a penalty.

I was under pressure from Martin Buchan and Alan Hansen but I kept my place for the game with Austria – Frankie Gray, Archie Gemmill and Robbo were also in the 20-man squad - at Hampden Park but Hans Krankl silenced the Hampden Roar five minutes before the break when Rough failed to reach a through ball.

Gordon McQueen played well that day (his best tackle was saved for a spectator who ran onto the pitch) and we thoroughly deserved Archie Gemmill's equaliser.

I didn't think I had played too badly, but that was me done until 1981.

Stein became a national icon, but I didn't rate him as a manager at all. But at least he had the good sense to recall me for the World Cup qualifier in Israel. Rough played well for once and we snatched it with a 53rd minute goal from Dalglish following a Robertson corner.

But Rough was injured in the next game against Northern Ireland and Billy Thompson came on. Steve Archibald hit the woodwork before Wark equalised after I made way for Hartford.

My final game was in the 2-0 Home International defeat by Wales at Swansea. Joe Jordan was sent off after clashing with Terry Boyle who suffered a broken nose. He also lost a tooth. It's probably still embedded in Joe's elbow.

Stein was a bit strict and didn't like us drinking. He didn't do much, he just strolled about most of the time. He was a bit sombre and I don't think I ever saw him smile.

I have to say he wasn't my cup of tea…which was about all he let us drink. I don't know why, but we never really got on at all and I only played a couple of times for him.

It's a good job he never bumped into me that day at Kings Cross station. I was with John Robertson and got so drunk on Vodka-lime that they wouldn't let me on a plane. Robbo dragged me into a taxi to the station and left me to go and buy two tickets for the sleeper. He had to drag me up a ramp and worked up a bigger sweat than he ever did playing football.

Unfortunately, in the distance we could hear football fans chanting. It turned out they were Man United fans and, as luck would have it, they spotted me. "Kenny Burns is Pissed" went up the chant. Fighting mad, I was ready to take them on three at a time.

Scotland had some great players, some world class, but they never really gelled as a team. I could never understand that because good players should be able play anywhere. And, at the end of the day, we all play on the same bit of grass.

At least we had some fun when we were playing for Scotland. Once I borrowed a car from Forest, an Austin Princess, it went from 0-60 in three days. Willie Johnson, who didn't drive, suggested we went to Perth Races and we had a good day up there. Then me, Willie, Derek Johnson and Don Masson met some birds. I was pissed as a fart driving and went straight through a detour and the car was badly damaged. Somehow, I managed to talk my way out of that one. I think I said we must have hit a rabbit or something.

On another occasion I almost wiped out half the Forest team driving up to Glasgow for a Scotland match. There was me and Robbo, with Archie stretched out asleep on the back seat. Suddenly a big wagon pulls out in front of us and I had to swerve to miss it. We ended up in the fast lane facing the oncoming traffic. Robbo almost wet himself and Archie slept with one eye open after that.

I'm sorry to say that I've been banned a couple of times for drink driving. It's not something I'm proud of. When I was at Leeds, I used to play in a local snooker league and got pie and chips to eat on the way home one night. I stuck my finger in the pie, which was red hot, and burnt my finger. The upshot was that the car hit a bollard and a nice lady asked me in for a cup of tea while I calmed down.

Unfortunately, a 'concerned member of the public' called the police. The upshot was that I was arrested and spent the night in a cell. It wasn't nice, but I've slept in worst places in Ilkeston. The next morning I was up before the beak and he banned me for a year.

The other time followed one of Forest' famous Christmas parties. I was driving home a bit the worst for wear when I got a puncture but I couldn't find the spare. I don't think I could have changed it anyway. I drove home from Wollaton Park on the rims and there were sparks flying everywhere. Of course, I got stopped by the police.

I'm not proud of my record. I wasn't very clever and I know I should have set a better example, but I don't think it makes me a bad person. I don't drink and drive anymore. I've learned my lesson.

Playing for Scotland was certainly a different experience from playing at club level and the opposition had dirty tricks that even I hadn't thought of. In one game, against Spain, I was waiting for a corner to be taken when this boy grabs my long hair. He lost two teeth as a result but my hand was killing me. One of the lads said: "It didn't take you long to get into the game did it?" It wasn't something I'm proud of. It's the darker side of the game. But, as I have said before, you can't allow people to bully you on the pitch.

Once, we had a good result in Norway and I went drinking with Joe Jordan and Gordon McQueen, who were big mates. I got absolutely legless. Joe was very quiet off the field but he was an animal on it.

We were running up and down the corridors like idiots and I was phoning everyone I could think of.

Willie Ormond liked a drink himself, so he didn't mind the players drinking. I never rated him. He never talked tactics and knew very little about the opposition – mind you, Brian Clough never bothered about the opposition either.

I only played 20 times for my country, which is something I regret. I should have done better; Scotland never saw the best of Kenny Burns. It hurt me that I lost my place to Tam Forsyth, a player Tommy Docherty had described as a "cart-horse." He was a wholehearted, gutsy player but he was short on ability. I felt let down. I never thought on myself as a world-class player like Baxter or Law, but I liked to think that I could play a bit.

The trouble with the Scottish-based players in the team is that the standard in Scotland is not good enough. It's poor – and it's falling all the time, with more and more foreigners coming in. There is always talk about Celtic and Rangers joining the Premier League – but, believe me, they would probably struggle to win the Championship.

I should have won more caps. I've only got one left now, which is in a case in my house. I gave the rest away to my sons and mates.

I was thinking of selling some of my shirts. But I would never sell my medals, or the replica cup that Brian Clough had made for us. You would have to blow me up to get them.

I am proud of every trophy I've won. I've still got the wee medals from my schooldays tucked away in a draw somewhere. What's the use of entering something unless to want to win it?

The most you win at the monthly medal at the golf club is £25 –
but it's a competition and I just have to win it. I love my golf these
days. After all, it's the only exercise I get. I can't be bothered with
going to the gym and that; it's so boring. And swimming is out - I got
banned from the baths for "bombing".

When I was at Forest, I was a member at Rushcliffe. Ron Hulme
got me involved in celebrity golf for the Variety Club. We used to go
up to events in his Rolls Royce. Now Ron, who had a snooker club
in Nottingham, knew everybody. Once, we were playing at Beeston
Fields. I was waiting to tee off on the 10th when this figure came
into view. I shouted "Four" but he kept on coming. He looked a big
bloke so I had second thoughts about making a fuss. When he got a
few yards away I recognised who it was - Sir Henry Cooper. He had
come looking for Ron and followed us around the course.

I'm currently a member at a smashing club, Kedleston Park, near
Derby, and I play as often as I can. It's a big part of my sporting, and
social life. John Webster is what you might call our social secretary,
mainly because he has a karaoke machine in his basement. He loves
singing Roy Orbison songs – but he's hopeless. I've heard worse on
X-Factor, but you have to say that the man is not blessed.

Some people think Kedleston Park is for snobs, because the likes
of millionaires, doctors and surgeons play there, but it's not. We are a
right mixed bunch. It's not quite the same banter that we used to get
playing football, but we get in a corner of the bar and have some fun
and take the piss out of each other.

Everyone is judged the same whether you have got a million or
two bob. Even if it's only for a few quid and a poxy little trophy, I
have to win. I play golf with three old Derby players Gerry Daly,
Billy Hughes and Rod Thomas and they'll tell you that I'm a
nightmare. Rod's not a great player by the way, but he's a good
drinker.

I balance golf with my public speaking and media work these
days. I really get a kick out of my media work and public
appearances – especially if they involve a reunion with some of the
lads. I love the reunions, any excuse to see the lads and talk about old
times is all right with me. It's like a kid's party when we all get

together. We had a question and answer session in Nottingham that 2,000 fans turned up for. It was an unbelievable night, 2,000 people to see old farts like us.

I also do after-dinner speaking and it's something I really enjoy. Everywhere I go people want to know about Brian Clough.

And I get a lot of satisfaction from doing my weekly column for the local Nottingham paper, the Evening Post. Garry Birtles also does one.

We were also involved in a popular radio show with Darren Fletcher, which was good fun. I never thought for one minute that end up doing this kind of thing because I always thought I would be a manager one day. But it's an aspect of the game that I thoroughly enjoy.

I particularly enjoyed the radio phone in. It used to be big Larry's show until David Platt, who was Forest manager then, complained about him and he was dropped.

Then I was asked to do it along with Garry Birtles, who was selling fish at the time and Alan Birchnall from Leicester. They used to give me a lift to the show when I was banned. In fact they carried on giving me lifts for about six months after the ban had finished – I just forgot to tell them.

We were like the Three Amigos until Roger Davies came in to provide the Derby County angle. Like Larry, I like to be honest and tell it how it is. I merely gave my opinion. We used to have a right laugh. When I used to have a wee dig at Derby the phone lines would soon light up. I don't think Roger was too happy either but he looked at it through blinkered eyes. Garry and I fell out on the radio. I think there is too much football on television, it is killing the game. But he makes his living from it now so he is bound to disagree. He is doing well on Sky. He's done well for himself. Good luck to him.

Feb 27 v Wales U-23 (Aberdeen, 5,900) 3-0
Stewart (Brown), Forsyth, Wallace, Robinson, Johnstone, Burns, Parlane, Kelly, Pearson, Cropley, Prentice (Doyle). Scorers: Parlane (pen), Robinson, Pearson.

1976

Feb 18 v Holland U-23 (Breda, 14,000) 0-2
Rough, Brownlee, McLelland, Miller, McVie (Narey), Souness, Burns, Bremner, J Craig, Dalglish, Johnstone.

1974

March 27, v West Germany (Frankfurt, 62,000) 1-2
Allan, Jardine, A Forsyth, Hay*, Buchan, Stanton, Morgan, Dalglish, Law, Hutchinson, Burns (Robinson). Scorer: Dalglish.

Oct 30 v East Germany (Hampden Park, 39,445) 3-0
Harvey, Jardine*, A Forsyth, Souness, Holton (Burns), Buchan, Johnstone (J), Dalglish (D Johnstone), Deans, Jordan, Hutchinson. Goals: Hutchinson (pen), Burns, Dalglish.

Nov 20 v Spain (Hampden Park, 92,100). 1-2
Harvey, Jardine, A Forsyth, McQueen, Burns, Bremner*, Souness, Hutchinson (Dalglish), J Johnstone, Deans (Lorimer), Jordan. Scorer: Bremner

1975

Feb 5 v Spain (Valencia, 60,000) 1-1
Harvey, Jardine, McQueen, Buchan, McGrain, Bremner*, Cooke, Hutchinson, Dalglish, Jordan (Parlane), Burns (Wilson). Scorer: Jordan.

1976

Oct 13 v Czechoslovakia (Prague, 38,000) 0-2
Rough, McGrain, Donachie, Buchan, McQueen, Rioch, Dalglish (Burns), Masson (Hartford), Jordan, A Gray, Gemmill.*

Nov 17 v Wales (Hampden Park, 63,233) 1-0
Rough, McGrain, Donachie, Blackley, McQueen, Rioch (Hartford), Burns, Dalglish, Jordan, Gemmill*, E Gray (Pettigrew). Scorer: Evans og.

1977

April 27 v Sweden (Hampden Park 22,659) 3-1
Rough, McGrain, T Forsyth, Blackley (Narey), Donachie, Glavin (Jardine), Dalglish*, Hartford, Burns (J Craig), Pettigrew, Johnston. Scorers: Hartford, Dalglish, Craig.

May 28 v Wales (Wrexham, 14,468) 0-0
Rough, McGrain, Donachie, Rioch*, (Johnston), McQueen, T Forsyth, Masson, Gemmill, Parlane (Burns), Dalglish, Hartford.

1978

May 13 v N Ireland (Hampden Park, 64,433) 1-1
Rough, Jardine, Buchan (Burns), T Forsyth, McQueen, Rioch, Masson,

Gemmill, Jordan (Dalglish), D Johnstone, Robertson. Scorer: Johnstone.

May 17 v Wales (Hampden Park, 70,241) 1-1

Blyth, Kennedy, Donachie, Burns, McQueen (T Forsyth), Gemmill*, Souness, Hartford, D Johnstone, Dalglish, Johnston (Robertson). Scorer: Johnstone.

May 20 v England (Hampden Park, 83,319). 0-1

Rough, Kennedy, Burns, T Forsyth, Donachie, Rioch* (Souness), Masson (Gemmill), Hartford, Dalglish, Jordan, Johnston.

June 3 v Peru (Cordoba, 47,000). 1-3

Rough, Burns, Kennedy, Forsyth, Buchan, Rioch* (Macari), Masson (Gemmill), Hartford, Dalglish, Jordan, Johnston. Scorer: Jordan.

June 7 v Iran (Cordoba, 10,000) 1-1

Rough, Buchan (T Forsyth), Jardine, Burns, Donachie, Macari, Gemmill*, Hartford, Jordan, Dalglish (Harper), Robertson. Scorer: og.

1979

June 7 v Norway (Oslo, 17,269)4-0

Rough, Burley (Hegarty) (Wark), Munro, Burns, McQueen, Gemmill*, Graham, Dalglish, Jordan, Hartford, Robertson. Scorers: Jordan, Dalglish, Robertson, McQueen.

Sept 12 v Peru (Hampden Park, 41,035) 1-1

Rough, Jardine*, Munro, Souness, McQueen, Burns, Cooper (Aitken), Wark (Graham), Dalglish, Hartford, Robertson. Scorer: og.

Oct 17 v Austria (Hampden Park, 72,700) 1-1

Rough, Jardine, Munro, Souness, McQueen, Burns, Wark, Gemmill*, Dalglish, Graham (Cooper), Robertson. Scorer: Gemmill.

Dec 19 v Belgium (Hampden Park, 25,389) 1-3

Rough, Jardine*, McGrain, Wark, McQueen, Burns, Dalglish, Aitken, D Johnstone, Bannon (Provan), Robertson. Scorer: Robertson.

1981

Feb 25 v Israel (Tel Aviv, 35,000) 1-0

Rough, McGrain, F Gray, Souness, McLeish, Burns, Wark (Miller), Dalglish (A Gray), Archibald, Gemmill*, Robertson. Scorer: Dalglish

March 25 v N Ireland (Hampden Park, 78,444) 1-1

Rough (Thomson), McGrain, F Gray, Burns (Hartford), McLeish, Miller, Wark, Archibald, A Gray, Gemmill*, Robertson. Scorer: Wark.

May 16 v Wales (Swansea) 0-2

Rough, Burns, Stewart, F Gray (McGrain), McQueen, Miller, Hartford*, Narey, Jordan, Provan, Graham (Sturrock).

Larking around with Rod Stewart before the World Cup

Having a sing-song with Rod and the boys

The Scotland squad before they left for Argentina

Brian organises a Highland fling with his Scottish Forest players

Me, Robbo and the Scotland squad

Archie Gemmill, John Robertson and myself

Jock Stein supervises a Scotland training session

Scotland v England. Trevor Francis

My hero. Jim Baxter

My one remaining Scotland cap

With my sons, Paul and Mark

Regrets

I've had a few - mainly concerning my kids. I think the world of all my kids. My love for them will never change. I've got three lovely daughters, Emma, Laura and Rachel, but Emma and Laura never sent me Fathers' Days cards or anything like that.

I married my first wife, Pat, at 17 while I was at Birmingham. She gave me two great lads, Mark and Paul, but we always struggled with money. I have to admit that I was not great with money; I had trouble keeping it in my pocket, especially when I was gambling.

I wish I could have been more like Robbo. He planned ahead and put every penny of his bonus money into a pension. I never bothered. I only planned for today. If I could give one piece of advice to a young apprentice these days it would be follow Robbo's example. Get a pension, even if it's only £5 a week.

Being a Scot I'm obviously careful with money now. No way I'm going to get into debt. The only money I owe is a mortgage on my house in Derby.

It helps, of course, when you win over £111,000 on the lottery like I did a couple of years ago. I couldn't believe it when I checked my numbers in the front room that Sunday morning. Five, plus the bonus ball. Bloody hell!

I went to the local paper shop and they said they would have to contact head office. I went shopping and spent £30 in the sales on things for the house. Then I rang a few friends and arranged to meet them at the golf club. We had a few celebration drinks and went for a meal at a place at Weston-on-Trent. Then Camelot called and I arranged to travel down to pick up the cheque.

I had money problems at Birmingham, that's for sure. I had started betting more and it all came to a head when I went to the club to ask them for a sub. They put me in touch with a chap called Keith Sales. When the bills came in I sent them to Keith to sort out. He'd send me a cheque for £110 every fortnight. I'd cash it and give the missus £80 for housekeeping. But, on a couple of occasions I gambled the lot away. Now I've always enjoyed a bet. At one time I'd bet on anything. It's stupid really, after all you never see a poor bookie do you?

Some of the players at Forest got into deep water with the bookies and it almost ruined Peter Shilton. I didn't realise how much until I did a bit of scouting for him when he was Plymouth manager. He sent me to run the rule over Mick Quinn in a game at Leicester.

I was used to working with hard-working strikers like Peter Withe, Tony Woodcock and Garry Birtles. But Mick, who was well into his horse racing, looked as though he had eaten the horse. Let's just say he didn't do a deal. Frankly, I was more impressed with a young lad called Phil Gee, who Derby County fans will know all about.

I put my report in advising against Quinn, so you can imagine my surprise a couple of days later when I saw the headline: "Plymouth sign Quinn." I'm sure Shilts only bought him so he could get some racing tips. He made a right pigs ear of things at Plymouth. Mind you, I can't think of too many ex-keepers, apart from Peter Taylor, who have done well in management, can you?

I still love a night at the dogs. I was brought up around greyhounds and used to walk them for my brothers. I slept in the same bed as a greyhound and I even ended up owning one, Fhlea Daz, which I got from Mr and Mrs Coppin. It was rubbish. It used to stop at the first bend to sign autographs and pose for pictures.

I play poker on line now and enjoy that. But I can take it or leave it. I'm older and wiser now and, unlike some players today, it's not a problem.

The Premiership players these days have so much money they don't know what to do with it. They are bored to tears; they don't know what to do with their free time and they gamble because they need that buzz.

In 1973-74 I went away with Birmingham pre-season and never went back to Pat at our semi in Tamworth. She probably still thinks I'm still on tour. But it wasn't Pat's fault; it was mine. I still see her from time to time. I've also met the family at weddings and the like. It's not a problem. It's all water under the bridge.

At the end of the day, I took the coward's way out. Yes, I was young, but I should have known better. It's not something I'm proud of and I felt very sorry for deserting the lads, Mark and Paul, who were only four and two.

I would take them out in the car for the day but there would be tears all round when it came time to take them back. I could see their faces pressed against the window and I would sit in the car crying my eyes out. It was hell. It was tearing me apart. I was numb. You could have run me through with a knife and I wouldn't have felt anything, so I decided it was best not to see them.

I convinced myself it was for the best; that I was being cruel to be kind. I was ashamed of myself and I missed out on seeing my two boys grow up – although they didn't do too badly without me.

I still see the boys now, they live in Birkenhead and Birmingham, and with time, they understood why I buggered off. I talk to them on the phone about football. They are football daft. Paul manages a team on Sunday mornings. He was a good little player and was offered trials with a couple of clubs but he couldn't drive at the time. And he likes a drink with the lads after a game.

Mark, my eldest, is a football buff. He knows everything about football. He is a big Manchester United fan – I can't forgive him for that. They've given me three grand-daughters but I don't see as much of them as I should do.

My second wife was Louise Onions, who I meet when I was asked to open her dad's sports shop in Tamworth, but we weren't an item or anything then. Her father, Eric Smith, had played for Leicester City and was an ex-bookie. He was a great chap and I got on really well with him.

One thing led to another and I spent the rest of my time at Birmingham with her. She came with me when I moved to Forest. We had two lovely daughters, Emma and Laura. Unlike Pat, she had all the good times – and the money. Because of her I hardly saw my boys, because it always led to arguments. I was warned by friends that she was a gold-digger but I took no notice. Looking back, she was a stuck-up little bitch.

I thought we were making a go of it in the pub at first but when the money ran out, so did she. I think she got involved with a toy boy; I suppose it made her feel young again.

But she stuck the knife in and that really hurt me. She left me in a right mess. Emma came to live with me in the pub but her mum sneaked in the backdoor and took her away one day. It was a very, very sad moment. Because, as her dad, I would have liked to bring her up. It would have been hard and I would have had to change my ways, I'm under no illusions about that. But I would have made sacrifices for her.

Afterwards, Louise told some friends that she had been unhappy for two or three years. I realise now that she only stayed because she was comfortable. Nice holidays, plenty of money.

I didn't see the girls because she blackened my name with them. She would answer the phone and say: "Your rotten father's on the phone." I still refer to her as Louise the bitch.

I am very bitter about her to this day. I want nothing to do with the bitch at all. If she came begging I would tell her to piss off – or something like that.

I got together with wife No3, Kath, on the re bound after Louise left me. I was low and drinking too much and, I suppose, I was lonely. Kath came to work for me in the pub and after calling time we'd sit and talk and have a drink. She was about ten years younger than me, but we got on well. One night a couple of drinks led to a couple of kisses and then a cuddle and one thing led to another. We were married in Burton and had the reception at the Barn Owl at Marchington.

When I left the pub I got a job playing for Ilkeston and working for their chairman. I was having to drive over from Uttoxeter and I was out from 6am to 6pm and it was getting a bit much for me. We started rowing and I was still drinking, but not as much.

In the end, I think it was the age gap that did it and we split up. But one good thing did come out of the marriage. Our beautiful daughter, Rachel, who is my little princess

While I was working in Ilkeston I got friendly with a receptionist, whose husband had died. That went sour when I found out she had been out for a drink with an ex-boyfriend. That was it. She was finished. Gone. She bombarded me with telephone calls after that, but I wasn't interested.

The new lady in my life, Jean, is different class. I was introduced to her by a mutual friend at a golf do and we became good friends. She's great. I can't speak too highly of her. She's one of the kindest people I have ever met and will do anything for anybody. The only trouble is she can't sit still for five minutes. She is always on the go, tidying up, moving furniture or washing something. I love my food and she is a great cook. She loves things like liver and onions and steak and kidney pie and spoils me to death.

Another regret is that I never performed better in a Scotland shirt and I also regret that I didn't get on better with referees throughout my career. I think they had it in for me from an early age. For some reason, sticking the nut on players seemed to upset them. Mainly I got booked for dissent though. That stopped when I went to Forest. Cloughie wouldn't tolerate arguing with referees – even if they were in the wrong. If you got booked for talking back to referees he fined you. Simple as that. In my first season at Forest I probably had more points on my driving licence.

I don't condone swearing at referees, it is just that I was so passionate about the game. I had this mad desire to win, sometimes at all costs.

I can't play anything for fun. When I play Connect 4 with the grand children I make sure I win. They are five and nine.......

One referee booked me for a late tackle. I told him I'd got there as quick as I could, but it didn't raise a laugh. On another occasion we were playing piggy-in-the-middle in the multi-gym before a game when a referee, who shall remain nameless, came up to me and said "I'm having you today." I thought Great. He was a true to his word. I went into a tackle, kicked out a little bit… and he sent me off.

You have probably gathered that I'm not a big fan of referees.

Ref's don't know what a tackle is these days. Not enough of them have played the game. If they had they would realise that it is a man's game. At least it used to be….

Jean, one of the kindest people I have ever met

Family and friends

Life after football...

With sons Paul and Mark

Mark and me at a family gathering

Rachel

Emma and Laura

Rachel

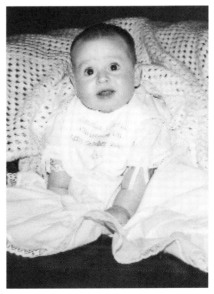

Granddaughters Rebecca and Amelia

Granddaughter Chloe

Chloe and Rebecca

Samuel, Elliot and Scarlet

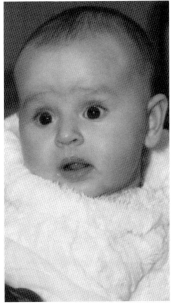

Amelia

Like many footballers, golf has been my passion since giving up the Beautiful Game

Willie Smith, at a 40-year reunion

Derby County's annual golf day 2006

The Iliffe Cup, Coventry Golf Club, September 2000

With Bill Loomes, Guy Oates and Andy Nelson

Nottingham Forest golf day

Burns Night

Subscribers

1   Charles Wheeler
2   Peter R Mitchell
3   John Whitehead
4   Paul Ludlow
5   Vic Heppenstall
6   Ron Brunton
7   Brian Parkin
8   Frank Woollatt
9   Gary Lambert
10 Martin Davis
11 Roy Pilkington
12 Chris Fagg
13 Ray Betts
14 May Selby
15 Anthony Ford
16 Stephen Purdy
17 Barrie Fell
18 Gary Hopewell
19 Scott Davies
20 Philip Sims
21 Alan Smith
22 Neil Hardstaff
23 Neal Baxter
24 Jim Parnham
25 Paul Andrews
26 Mark Greatorex
27 Neil Atkins
28 Alan Fells
29 Paul Matthews
30 Carol Kerslake
31 Darren Craggs
32 Terry Turner
33 Rupert Bellamy
34 Pauline Wilkinson

35 Ted Smith
36 Craig Huckle
37 Neil R.Smith
38 Richard Burgess
39 Simon Giddens
40 T.O. Marsden
41 Robin Dale
42 Tim Gough
43 Steven Fox
44 Ben
45 Roy
46 Alan Clarke
47 Simon Geeson
48 Adrian Killer
49 John Charles Spencer
50 John Hanbury
51 Kevin Cumberland
52 Stephen Hill
53 Peter Smith
54 Jason Cliff
55 Francis Eizens
56 Matthew Elson
57 Barry Smith
58 Alan Wallhead
59 Richard H Harrison
60 Ian Daubney
61 Darren Boden
62 Mark Jackson
63 Ivor Gibbs
64 Ivan
65 Brad Herod
66 Roger Dickinson Driving School
67 Michael Beardsmore

68	Shaun	104	Jim Hyson
69	Jason	105	Mark Garton
70	Chris	106	Richard & Jane
71	Adrian Straw	107	Dave
72	Harry Grantham	108	Susan
73	Alex Grantham	109	Big Tony
74	Richard Parker	110	Linda
75	M Andrew	111	Wilson Howden
76	Mike Harris	112	Kim Upton
77	Iain	113	John Plevey
78	Monkeyman	114	Chris Odell
79	Tony Cuttell	115	Kevin Cooper
80	Julie Haynes	116	Alex Buck
81	John Brian Baxter	117	Simon Robinson
82	Glyn Moxham	118	Matt Robinson
83	David Day	119	Norman Balmer
84	Simon Bingham	120	Pete W
85	Mark Bingham	121	Joe
86	Matt Dobson	122	Joe
87	Joe Dobson	123	Paul
88	Wayne Armstrong	124	Wayne
89	Clive Ratcliffe	125	Bill
90	Mark Davidson	126	Malcolm
91	Trevor Fermie	127	Colin
92	David	128	Mick Turland
93	Kevin Ward	129	Paul, Aimie, Rebecca & Chloe
94	Malcolm		
95	Gary Marriott	130	Mark, Jacquie & Amelia
96	Carol Courtney	131	Andrew Oates
97	Pete Washington	132	Guy Oates
98	Christopher Brooks	133	Mark Shinfield
99	David & Nick Long	134	Andy
100	Martin	135	Max
101	Chris Nye	136	Lofty
102	Sarah Harvey	137	Paul J Anderson
103	Barbara Barley	138	Darrell Bowser

139 Adrian Buck
140 Richard Jones
141 Stuart Kaye
142 Carl Ellson
143 Wayne
144 Allan Allsop
145 Guy Smith
146 Andrew Dilkes
147 John Hutchinson
148 Pete Brown
149 Neil Buck
150 Leslie Hart
151 Paul Kirk
152 Paul James
153 Martin
154 Michael
155 Frank Campbell
156 Jason Campbell
157 Paul Morley
158 Tom Jones
159 Paul Brogan
160 Chris Davies
161 Tim Bennett
162 Bernard Brogan
163 Pauline Webster
164 Andrew Sterling
165 Bill Sterling
166 Xanthi & Johnny Ferguson
167 Paul Rhodes
168 Steve Beckett
169 Barry Turner
170 Neil Hesseltine
171 Paul Thomas
172 Mrs Webb
173 Dave Trussell
174 Duncan Horton

175 Paul Hughes
176 Brian Corry
177 Paul Evans
178 Paul BCFC
179 John James Middlemass
180 Malc
181 Kevin Reidy
182 James
183
184 Dominic Hammond
185 William Mairs
186 Mary & Tony
187 David Martin
188 John Martin
189 Alan
190 Terry Rossington
191 Roy Jinks
192 Keith Brace
193 David Bamford
194 Dave Shaw
195 Sean Kehoe
196 Nick Pritchett
197 Mick Sherry
198 Colin Wiltshire
199 Darren Taylor
200 Steve Cook
201 David Cook
202 Nora Charity
203 Terry Thorne
204 Steve Knowles
205 Jamie Smith
206 Andrew
207 Shane Barnes
208 Kevin Stringer
209 Malcolm Nix
210 Steve Giles

211 Archie Brown
212 AG Bourne
213 Lizzie
214 Simon Cooper
215 Trev
216 Kevin Meredith
217 Bert Blyth
218 Tony
219 Kev
220 Andrew Poole
221 Malc
222 David Pearson
223 Paul
224 Peter Courts
225 Joseph Such
226 Ian Newman
227 Andrew George
228 Andy
229 Colin Williams
230 Brian Handley
231 Steve
232 Simon